The key to your
Dreams

Tamara Trusseau

NH
NEW
HOLLAND

154.63
TRU

First published in 2008 by
New Holland Publishers (UK) Ltd
London • Cape Town • Sydney • Auckland
Text copyright © 2008
New Holland Publishers (UK) Ltd
Copyright © 2008 New Holland Publishers (UK) Ltd

Garfield House
86–88 Edgware Road
London W2 2EA
www.newhollandpublishers.com

80 McKenzie Street
Cape Town 8001
South Africa

Unit 1, 66 Gibbes Street
Chatwood
NSW 2067
Australia

218 Lake Road
Northcote
Auckland
New Zealand

ISBN 978 1 84773 059 6

Senior editor   Corinne Masciocchi
Designer   Sue Rose
Artworks   Tamara Trusseau
Production   Hazel Kirkman
Editorial direction   Rosemary Wilkinson

Reproduction by Modern Age Repro, Hong Kong
Printed and bound by Leo Paper Products, China

1 3 5 7 9 10 8 6 4 2

Contents

Introduction

Since the beginning of time, dreams have provoked and aroused great curiosity and debate. While there are many historical references to the mystical and divinatory aspects of dreams, in more recent times, the emphasis has been primarily on psychological significance. Whether prophetic or subconscious analogy, the interpretation of dreams can provide great insight into past, present and future. Dreams hold the key to unlocking and understanding one's fears, obstacles and traumas as well as providing clarification to otherwise inaccessible situations.

In certain cultures and religions, including some Native American tribes and aspects of Mayan and Aztec traditions, dreams are considered the shadow of reality where hopes and fears are assessed and evaluated before being manifested physically. The concept of the shadow is expanded further, enabling dreams to be considered 'reality', while conscious interaction becomes 'illusion'. According to tribal beliefs, this inner knowledge is a reflection of where reality is born and since knowledge begins deep in the subconscious, dreams contain intriguing fragments and images that liberate and exhibit the truth.

Of course, due to the fascinating complexities of the mind, dreams occur in symbolic form. Although at times these symbols may appear irrational and unconnected to everyday life, they generally stem from one's own experiences, knowledge and beliefs. The archives of the mind often provide the resources from which, after some manipulation and careful editing, the appropriate dream may be derived. The basis for the construction of a dream would also be heavily dependent on the needs of the subject. Whether fulfilling a wish, facing a fear, dealing with an uncomfortable situation or answering challenging questions, the purpose of dreaming is to provide knowledge and understanding.

Dreams may be divided into distinct categories and as every impression has a reason for being integrated into a particular setting, the importance of investigation and

detailed analysis is evident. The only exception occurs when images have been induced or manipulated by physical causes. For instance, should a subject be bitten by an insect while asleep and dreaming, the event may be incorporated and translated into the dream under an alternative format. The feeling of pain and the location on the body where the bite occurred would remain constant but the action portraying this incident would be composed and assembled differently. In the dream, the insect can be represented by a number of potential replacements and although the pain would be undoubtedly real, the cause of the sensations may have been distorted into a sequence of scenarios, generated for the sole purpose of adjusting to environmental conditions. Clearly, where such external physical influences come into play, the meaning is self-explanatory and requires no further probing.

The most important point to consider while dissecting any dream is that communication has been provoked by the subconscious for a reason. The curious impressions conveyed serve to create harmony, restore balance, maintain order and offer advice where the conscious mind has not succeeded in deducing satisfactory answers. By understanding the significance of different genres of dream and taking into consideration the possible motives behind the formation of such images, immense clarity and definition can be attained. Above all, dreams are honest portrayals of reality, conceived and designed with tremendous care and deliberation in an effort to instigate insight, judgment and greater perception.

Dream categories

*D*reams may be divided into different categories. While communication remains the basis for all dreams, it is motivation that creates the categories. The subconscious goes through great lengths to convey relevant and effective pictures. There is a specific reason behind every image dreamed and so it may be concluded that dreams are induced by events and emotions that are of significant bearing and interest. As the enormous power of the subconscious extends into different realms of activity, this inevitably gives rise to a diverse group of dreams. Whether driven by the need to sift through recent events and create order out of chaos, or delve into the archives of the mind to confront unresolved issues, the common denominator remains an instinctive desire to eliminate problems and reach a constructive conclusion.

Psychological dreams

This particular type of dream is usually induced by the subconscious as it tries to analyse recent events and suggest viable solutions. Quite often, the images contain characters and experiences from everyday life. By using these familiar settings, the subconscious recreates the situations in need of specific attention with the purpose of decoding the symbols so that they may offer practical answers. The most prominent objection associated with psychological dreams is the need to highlight the truth. Negatively charged situations containing stress and confusion can at times lead to a distorted understanding of a predicament. Psychological dreams assist in clarifying misguided perceptions by offering a truthful interpretation of hidden and unresolved conditions. (See pages 21–36 for case studies.)

Recurring dreams

Sometimes, the subconscious chooses to repeatedly display the same set of events. Such occurrence is usually provoked by long-held fears and traumas that have not been dealt with successfully. These types of dream should always be taken seriously. More often than not, the subject's emotional growth and development have been stunted and as a result emotional and psychological blockages have been formed. This delicate situation requires care and caution to resolve, and the fact that the subconscious is so determined to address the problem proves that the subject is ready to confront the difficulties and take the first step towards effective healing. (See pages 37–47 for case studies.)

Dreams prompted by physical and environmental conditions

In these types of dream, images have been manipulated as a result of external or physical influences. Whether provoked by indigestion, a change in room temperature or any other unexpected element, the result is then projected into the dream as it continues to affect the senses. As regards to such examples, further investigation is unnecessary as the meaning is clearly defined by the circumstances. (See pages 47–49 for case studies.)

Predictive dreams

These are perhaps the most mysterious of all dreams as they are very much based on intuition and premonition. The experiences associated with these types of dream feel different to all other formats. There is a heightening of senses and the events and emotions seem exceptionally real. The basis for these dreams lies within an instinctive urge to access what is normally considered remote and unattainable information. Ultimately, the main purpose of all predictive dreams is to provide unparalleled guidance and to help unravel curious and puzzling situations. (See pages 49–55 for case studies.)

Nightmares

The reasons behind the creation of such disturbing images cannot be generalised into one definitive format as nightmares can be produced within all categories of dreams. Since both pleasure and pain can be simultaneously induced for effect, nightmares may be regarded as an extreme form of communication. Whether associated with psychological conditions expressing fear or perhaps heightened premonition sensing danger, the underlying need is to shock the subject into action. Unless triggered by environmental conditions, nightmares portray a desperate attempt by the subconscious to highlight important issues, and these types of dream should therefore be treated with care and caution. (See pages 55–65 for case studies.)

Understanding the symbols

*D*reams may be regarded as a combination of impressions that have been carefully selected and brought together to provoke introspection and encourage understanding and communication. The meanings behind most symbols find their roots in universal beliefs and ideals. However, traditional values, cultural issues and personal experiences all contribute to create a distinct and very personal set of images. As it is highly improbable for two individuals to share identical experiences and emotions all through their lives, it can be safely assumed that every dream is unique and relevant to each individual.

However, while the personal elements within each dream cannot be ignored, many impressions derive from ideologies that have evolved with mankind. The link between certain symbols and their meaning is clear, as indicated in the following examples:

Forest = the unknown.
Egg = inspiration; new beginning.
Hatch = the onset of an interesting cycle.

The forest has an association with the unknown, as often it can appear mysterious and there is usually some uncertainty as to what dwells within. So potentially a change of circumstance that falls outside the boundaries of the tried and tested may, in a dream, be represented by a forest.

The egg can refer to the creation of a thought, notion or plan that can give rise to a new beginning. It is important to remember that the egg represents only the existence of a new idea and not necessarily the implementation of a concept into a tangible format. The meaning of each symbol can be quite specific so it is useful to remember as much detail as possible. For instance, should the egg hatch, it would imply that the plan is put into motion and a stimulating phase will ensue.

Examples of how a variation in detail can alter the meaning of a dream can be found in the differences between fly and airplane:

Fly = a desire to escape from the mundane.
Airplane = to fly in an airplane indicates outside help may be required to set oneself free from a binding situation.

To see oneself flying suggests a sense of fantasy and imagination. It also strongly awakens sensations of release and liberation. Should these ideas be applied to daily life, the overall interpretation suggests a need to break free from what feels like a rather banal existence.

To fly in an airplane, however, suggests that the flight is not based on fantasy but rather taking place with a craft specifically designed for the purpose. As flight is generally linked with freedom, it is logical to conclude that the inclusion of an airplane into the equation signifies the need for external influences to accomplish objectives.

Symbols as analogies

Many symbols highlight psychological and emotional issues in an attempt to offer constructive advice or criticism. In such cases, physical images are usually brought into play and the final result can appear to be a metaphor of the situation in question. For example:

Injury = disillusionment; disappointment in a relationship.
Hoard = a warning not to clutter the mind with unnecessary and potentially harmful thoughts.

Physical injuries in dreams are usually indicative of distress and disappointment. Such imagery relates to all types of attachments, including romantic involvements, family ties and close friendships. The correlation between emotional suffering and physical affliction finds its roots firmly embedded in the human psyche and history. The phrase 'mind over matter' is used frequently to emphasise the importance of thought and belief when combating physical ailments and attaining general wellbeing. As such it makes sense to assume that emotional distress can have physical associations within the mind. For instance, feeling hurt is commonly referred to as having a 'broken heart'. This form of analogy remains consistent across most cultures and has persisted throughout time.

In the 'hoard' example, the subconscious aims to highlight the consequences of a particular act by applying its principles to psychological conditions. Compulsive hoarding is not generally considered a healthy pastime. Excessively gathering objects is unnecessary and is often associated with deeper issues. The same applies to hoarding in a dream, only here the objects gathered represent negatively charged thoughts that affect the balance of the mind, and if left unchecked and unresolved on a conscious level can cause major upheavals and setbacks.

Word association

The link between words and their associations can be further highlighted with the following examples:

Abdomen = refers to 'gut' feeling. A pain in the abdomen is a warning not to ignore one's instincts.
Intestines = it is important to 'digest' all relevant information before reaching a decision.

In the case of abdomen, the subconscious plays on the correlation between this part of the body and instinctive feelings. With intestines the focus is on digestion, as that is the associated function and as such the subject is encouraged to examine any relevant material and 'digest' the information before taking further action.

At times the subconscious finds the need to accentuate truths and facts that may have lain dormant or escaped attention. In such cases the symbols often contain underground or hidden images as the situation is yet to fully surface. For example:

Mine = any mine- or mining-related dreams refer to talents and abilities yet to be discovered and put to use.

In the case of a mine, the deposits unearthed are normally of an extremely useful or desirable nature. Usually it takes time to discover such riches and considerable patience and expertise are required to ensure successful extraction. In a dream, the mine represents untapped potential that is yet to be fully explored and understood. However, the effort made by the subconscious to highlight the issue suggests that the time is right for further investigation. Consequently the process of discovery and application demands meticulous care and perseverance as any form of natural talent needs nurturing to reach its full potential.

More often than not, the key to understanding the images in a dream lies within the vast range of commonly held beliefs and ideals that expand into all aspects of everyday life. These can include folklore and superstition, as well as historical facts, social structure and political hierarchy. Popular conceptions about the natural world are also frequently incorporated into dreams. For example:

Elephant = nurturing instincts.
Cat = a more confidant and detached approach towards a partnership can instigate beneficial results.
Caterpillar = life-changing events.
Lion = family support.
Dolphin = playful endeavours; spiritual contentment.
Snake = false friends; betrayal.
Camel = the necessity for endurance and stamina.

The symbolic meaning of animals in dreams relates to a wide range of conduct including behavioural patterns, social interaction and general habits and characteristics. The above examples demonstrate the correlation between the symbol and its meaning as each animal exhibits attributes or beliefs commonly associated with it. However, not every link is dependent purely on mannerisms, disposition or environmental observation. At times, a person's perception of an animal triggers an alternative version of reality. In the case of the snake for instance, the meaning focuses on the concept of deceit and untrustworthy friendships. This has little to do with the conduct of the snake in the wild. Instead, the connection may be regarded as a derivative of related fears and feelings which have endured through time and have been legitimised by numerous references in literature and religion. An example of this can be found in the Bible; it is the serpent that destroys happiness and harmony in Eden through lies, manipulation and deception. The negative portrayal of the snake is such that even everyday expressions contain derogatory references: sleazy, slimy and sly are all adjectives associated with snakes and are used to describe a contemptible person or underhand behaviour.

Unlike the snake, the example of the dolphin concentrates on the positive associations that have developed through time. Whilst its playful disposition has been demonstrated, the spiritual connection has also continuously persisted, although this is not a tangible fact that can be scientifically proven. The dolphin may be regarded as an example of how the subconscious cleverly combines fact with theory, impression, doctrine or belief.

However, in all dreams, proper clarification relies on the analysis of as much detail as possible. In cases featuring animals, the interaction involved can be of tremendous importance, as demonstrated here:

Animals = any form of fun and enjoyment in relation to animals signifies peace and harmony. To be attacked by an animal is a sign of treachery and emotional discord; to hear animals suggests unexpected situations ahead; to feed animals emphasises the need for more compassion and understanding.

The link between animal, action and association is based on instinctive, spiritual and emotional principles. For instance, feeding an animal may be regarded as a rewarding gesture. Where appropriate, this correlation is then used by the subconscious to convey the need for greater kindness and generosity.

In the case of hearing an animal, the connection is based on instinct. Most animals have an acute awareness of changes in circumstance which is felt on an intuitive rather than sensory level. They can readily sense imminent situations and

react accordingly. Often, the response to such a predicament can include vocal elements, in the face of danger for example, or when confronted with unfamiliar conditions. Consequently, this particular reaction is selected by the subconscious as a symbol to highlight unforeseen situations.

This pattern of substitution is exercised within all dream categories. However, when it comes to the formulisation of symbols, it is perhaps in the arena of relationships that the mind produces some of its finest work. For example, a man may have a dream in which he is back with his ex-girlfriend. The likelihood of this being representative of a return to that actual relationship is remote. A more likely scenario would be that the subconscious has incorporated the ex-girlfriend to accentuate certain aspects of the relationship or as an indication of a new love interest. Should the latter option be the case, the fact that the ex-girlfriend symbolises the new love interest suggests that the two women share common qualities and characteristics.

At times the subconscious replaces one person with another in an attempt to provide important clues and highlight certain attributes. Initially, comparable traits, whether physical, emotional or psychological, as well as quirks in personality are closely examined and taken into consideration. Other factors such as place of birth, marital status and occupation are also analysed before the subconscious makes a choice. For example, a woman may dream of falling in love with a colleague. If in this case the colleague is representative of another man, one of the first observations would be that the new man may come through work. The physical characteristics of the colleague may also be relevant; perhaps the new love interest is of a similar height or has the same colour hair. Alternatively, it may be purely a question of personality; both men may share a great sense of humour or have a passion for music. Invariably, any choice made by the subconscious is inspired by motive and reason and a study of all the relevant possibilities can prove highly informative.

The bearing of external influences

The importance of personal experience in relation to the composition of dreams should not be neglected. Trauma and phobias in particular significantly affect the outcome of dreams and must be clarified and interpreted accordingly. For instance, should the subject experience a fear of travelling on an airplane, the usual correlations are no longer sufficient. As an object of dread, the plane cannot be merely used to convey its usual definition of liberation through external influences and its meaning must be adjusted to reflect personal association.

Perhaps the most compelling aspect of a dream lies within the intensity of emotional content. While most images represent conditions and situations, the accompanying sensations determine reaction and consequence. The emotions felt can seem very real and may be translated by a physical response such as tears, laughter, pain or palpitations. Although at the time the emotional provocation stems from the variables in the dream, the ensuing relevance of those feelings may be regarded as parallel to what would be experienced in reality. This further suggests that emotional ingredients almost act as a constant in relation to both imagery and interpretation. For example:

Joy = a period of peace and contentment.
Anger = anger in any form depicts difficulties; it also refers to inner struggle and guilt.
Happiness = a positive omen depicting triumph and pleasure.
Anxiety = doubts about one's own abilities.
Hate = any feelings of hatred refer to disruptive and undesirable relationships.
Distress = inner conflict and a longing to break free.
Pain = emotional disappointment.
Love = a dream of wish fulfilment, indicating a yearning for love and affection.
Lust = weakness; a questionable sense of judgement.
Anguish = indicates much doubt as regards an emotional situation.

An emotion experienced in a dream may be considered actual in reality. For instance, should the subject dream of being attacked by a snake and feel pain, anguish and distress, this would highlight a situation containing betrayal which would then lead to much doubt, conflict and a possible ending of a relationship. Upon closer inspection, it is obvious that the feelings experienced during the attack are no different to the emotions that would surface in reality should there be unexpected exposure to disloyalty and falsehood.

The fact that sentiments and physical sensations can originate in symbols and manifest into reality is an indication of the significance of emotional substance within dreams. While the imagination produces intriguing impressions using guidelines supplied by the subconscious, any associated meaning is further validated by an ingenious integration of feelings and sensitivities. With boundless limits and candid exposure, dreams convey truths and realities. Since knowledge is perceived as power, hidden within the symbolic world of dreams lies the key.

Interpreting your dreams

The ancient art of dream interpretation has been subject to much change and scrutiny throughout its controversial history. While dreams come into existence for a reason, the purpose and motivation behind the imagery can at times be shrouded in mystery. There are several reasons behind this ambiguity, the most evident being that the precise meaning of symbols can only be fully determined when they are considered not only individually but in conjunction with the subject's personal experiences and feelings towards them. After all, the boundaries between universally recognised symbolic correlation and personal circumstances are not always apparent. However, regardless of individual quirks, accurate interpretation is dependent on a mix of knowledge, imagination and instinct together with an understanding of the different dream categories. Any personal links and variations may be incorporated without any major adjustments to the original procedure. Although every detail in a dream yields valuable information, the following should be given special consideration:

• **Key images** These include aspects of the dream that seem particularly prominent. Usually, these are the elements most vividly remembered upon waking.

• **Emotions** All feelings and sensations experienced are of immense importance and should be examined carefully.

• **Sequence of events** The order in which images appear is also of significant interest as it can have a direct bearing on the final conclusion.

To demonstrate the technique behind successful dream interpretation, detailed case studies are featured along with a more thorough analysis of the dream categories. Each dream is also accompanied by additional information pertinent to the subject's personal circumstances to provide a more personalised analysis.

The most effective way to explore and evaluate a dream is to break it down into segments. These divisions should be made at points where there is a sense of transition, such as a change of setting, tempo, mood or any other obvious introduction of fresh elements. All key images and emotions should then be analysed in the context of the subject's personal circumstances.

Although the dictionary (see pages 66–126) examines many symbols, should an image from the dream not have an exact reference, a comparable word reflecting similar action or emotion can be applied instead. Where necessary, alternative words describing the same object may also be substituted. For instance, the dictionary contains the entry 'snake' but not 'serpent'. If in the dream the word serpent is used, turn to the snake entry to reveal its symbolic meaning.

Once all key images and emotions have been analysed, a glance at the sequence of events reveals further clues. All relevant information must be taken into account before arriving at an overall interpretation. It is also important to remember that certain types of dream operate outside the usual understanding of symbolic association. Examples relating to these, as well as all other dream categories, are included to provide greater insight

Psychological dreams

With psychological dreams the primary focus is to create balance and harmony by objectively confronting any pending issues and assessing desires and ambitions. The analysis can range from an investigation of disruptive emotional dilemmas to a candid review of potential career opportunities. Regardless of the subject matter, the aim is to provoke thought and contemplation and to provide a realistic and obtainable solution. Although quite often psychological dreams are induced by periods of upheaval and confusion, at times their purpose is directed solely towards offering alternative perspectives or revising long-held aspirations. Note that psychological dreams may regularly appear to have predictive undertones. These augural connotations are due to the instinctive observations associated with the subconscious and should not be confused with prophetic information. The following three examples represent common variations on this particular theme.

EXAMPLE A:
An in-depth observation of current issues

Subject: Jane

Background information: Jane is 38 years old. She is recently divorced after a long and problematic period of separation and feels reasonably confidant about entering into a new relationship. Through mutual friends, she has met Allen, whom she regards as a potential candidate. After just a few weeks Jane has started dwelling on the possibility of commitment. Although it has come to light that she is uncomfortable with some of Allen's opinions on fundamental issues, at this point she does not appear deterred.

Jane's dream

'I was walking along an isolated path until I reached what seemed to be a forest. By then it was night and I felt a little scared. I ventured slightly into the forest but not too far and then I saw a pond... I think there was a swan there as well. Next I found myself in a strange house. I went upstairs into a room that had a bed but I don't think it was the bedroom. I kept looking at the mattress and the pillows. They were a very strong shade of red. Then I went downstairs and in the kitchen there was a single red rose next to a knife on an old table. The rose smelt beautiful but somewhere in that kitchen there was something rotting and I could really smell it! It was horrible! I felt nauseous. I thought I should find whatever it is and throw it out. I couldn't find it and then the smell was everywhere and then I woke up...'

Analysis

This particular dream may be divided into three parts. The first section covers Jane's feelings on the divorce and her fears towards entering into a new relationship. The second part relates to a subconscious understanding of the new affair and the final segment is an analysis of Jane's hopes and anxieties and an exploration of the true possibilities in this relationship.

Part 1

'I was walking along an isolated path until I reached what seemed to be a forest. By then it was night and I felt a little scared. I ventured slightly into the forest but not too far and then I saw a pond... I think there was a swan there as well.'

Any form of walking is a reference to movement within the journey of life. This was taking place on an isolated path.

Walk = represents pace and movement through events and situations.
Path = depending on the other details seen in the dream, a path is representative of an important decision and its eventual consequences.

In Jane's case the path reflects the separation from her husband and the inevitability of divorce. The isolated path suggest that Jane has had to be on her own for a while and the underlying implication is that it has not been something that she has particularly enjoyed.

In the dream Jane then finds herself in a forest. She is suddenly aware that it is night and this fills her with a sense of fear.

Forest = the unknown.
Night = completion; ending.
Fear = any fear-related dreams usually point to unresolved emotional issues.

The forest represents the possibility of a new relationship. This is obviously an unknown territory and proves emotionally provocative. The fact that the night fills her with fear indicates that there are still unsettling elements relating to her previous marriage which she has not yet fully resolved. There is also an impression that to some degree these issues may be influencing her subconsciously, certainly in terms of her expectations relating to any new commitment. This is a very interesting point as consciously Jane seems very excited about the prospect of a new love interest. However, one of the major functions of psychological dreams is to highlight the truth and in this case it is clear that Jane has not yet confronted some of the deeper concerns associated with her divorce. Next in the dream, Jane decides to venture into the forest until she reaches a pond where there is also a swan.

Pond = a relationship that seems to be at a standstill.
Swan = an indication of faith and hope.

The pond is indicative of where the relationship stands at the moment between Jane and Allen. They have been seeing each other for a while, they have reached a certain point and now it feels as if everything has stopped while there is a review. The fact that Jane has only ventured slightly into the forest suggests that although she would like to be involved in a serious relationship, she is presently ruled by her insecurities. These could include a fear of rejection as well as doubts about Allen's intentions. However, as the swan offers faith and hope she is trying to be optimistic about any future prospects.

Part 2

'Next I found myself in a strange house. I went upstairs into a room that had a bed but I don't think it was the bedroom. I kept looking at the mattress and the pillows. They were a very strong shade of red.'

This section of the dream starts with another unfamiliar territory which is represented by a strange house.

House = more often than not, the house depicts the person, with the various rooms representing aspects of the personality as well as one's life in general.

For example, the kitchen relates to domestic matters, while the bedroom refers to love and relationship issues. The basement, however, can touch on secrets, fears and inhibitions. Different rooms must be looked at individually along with all other relevant details. To move house is a sign of transition and modification

The house represents Allen and the rooms are indicative of the different facets and features within the relationship. Since the house feels strange, it can be assumed that subconsciously Jane has questions and concerns which are further substantiated as the dream progresses.

Jane goes upstairs to enter a room. As she is visually aware of the stairs and her action, this points to an acceptance of certain difficulties and a readiness to confront them. Once in the room, she is aware of a bed and consequently, her initial reaction is to assume that she is in a bedroom. Yet she feels confused and unsure as to where she actually is. Since the bed represents a major decision and the bedroom highlights love matters, it can be assumed that Jane has reached an important point in the relationship, but her doubts as to the nature of the room indicate that she is uncertain about her next move.

Stairs = to go upstairs promotes a willingness to confront and surmount problematic situations; going downstairs highlights deep-rooted emotional insecurities that need time and patience to overcome.
Bed = an important decision.
Bedroom = the emphasis lies on love and relationship issues.
Room = an aspect of the personality.

Jane is then very much focused on the mattress and the pillows.

Mattress = material welfare.
Pillow = a superficial relationship.

It seems that the root of Jane's insecurities lies within a subconscious understanding of Allen's attitude towards love and relationships. At some point she must have observed that his current priority has a more financial and material orientation and that there is no present interest in a more serious involvement. The colour red confirms this further by reiterating Allen's need for passion which in itself does not necessarily include a desire for commitment.

Red = passion; instinctive energy.

Part 3

'Then I went downstairs and in the kitchen there was a single red rose next to a knife on an old table. The rose smelt beautiful but somewhere in that kitchen there was something rotting and I could really smell it! It was horrible! I felt nauseous. I thought I should find whatever it is and throw it out. I couldn't find it and then the smell was everywhere and then I woke up...'

Jane's decision to go downstairs reinforces the fact that she has not yet recuperated from the effects of her divorce although she is clearly trying to resolve any lingering issues. At this point the remainder of the dream may be followed in the kitchen.

Kitchen = refers to home and domestic matters, and depending on the other details involved, focuses on aspirations or problems in this area.
Rose = a token of love and affection.
Knife = represents actions and words that if used unwisely can cause great damage.
Old = to be aware of anything looking old or should any form of ageing be particularly poignant in a dream, the emphasis remains with time and the need to reach important targets within a certain period.
Table = purpose; intention.
Smell = to be aware of a pleasant smell denotes joy and gratification; an offensive smell points to a potentially damaging situation.
Rot = to see anything rotting suggests that swift action needs to be taken to initiate a productive change in the current course of events.
Nausea = inability to make certain emotional decisions.

Jane now finds herself in the kitchen which can be regarded as a reference to domestic and home-related issues. Since the dream so far has placed great emphasis on her feelings towards commitment, the kitchen may represent Jane's hopes and aspirations in terms of co-habitation. There she finds a single red rose next to a knife on an old table. The rose underlines Jane's need for love and in this instance the colour red highlights an instinctive desire to fulfil the romantic elements of her nature. However, she is very aware that it is a single red rose. The subconscious at times provokes a particular word in order to emphasise its importance. The use of the word 'single' in this case implies that Allen does not share Jane's romantic notions to the same degree.

The presence of the knife provides another clue to the current dynamics of this relationship. There is a suggestion that any actions or words utilised so far have not contributed to calming Jane's fears and anxieties as regards to the future. The knife

and the rose are on an old table emphasising the importance of time in terms of making all plans and intentions clear. The potential complexity of the situation is accentuated further with the existence of opposing odours. Whilst the rose smells beautiful, there is also something rotting in the kitchen. The contrast suggests that although Jane is enjoying aspects of this romantic interlude action needs to be taken to induce better definition and clarity as to the direction of this relationship. However, she also experiences nausea in this dream, which indicates that in her current state of mind, making decisions is not particularly easy or straightforward.

Finally, Jane makes an attempt to discover the source of this offensive odour but she does not succeed and instead wakes up feeling consumed by the smell. This implies that she is not looking in the right places to find the answers to her present dilemma and that until she changes her approach, it is unlikely that the situation will improve.

Conclusion

In this dream, Jane's subconscious primarily highlights two major concerns; firstly, whether Jane is ready for a serious involvement and secondly, even if the conditions were to be agreeable for such a major step, would Allen be an appropriate choice? Having examined the evidence offered by the subconscious there are misgivings in relation to both questions. While Jane continues with an inner struggle to heal painful emotional wounds, would an involvement with a man who has no serious intention help or hinder her personal battle? There are of course certain indications that Jane is enjoying aspects of this affair but her emotional fragility cannot be ignored. In this particular situation, unless a more productive approach is incorporated into the scenario, the likelihood of a satisfactory outcome is rather slim. Jane's vulnerability together with Allen's casual approach, do not form a comfortable blend and Jane's subconscious has made concise references to support the reasons behind this conclusion.

EXAMPLE B:
An objective exploration of hopes and fears

Subject: Ellen

Background information: Ellen is an interior designer in her early thirties. She is single, self-employed and may be considered highly ambitious. Despite some major achievements, recently she has felt rather restless and uncertain as to the direction of her career. Also, there has been some diversification of her views and beliefs with the arrival of renewed spiritual interest and psychic development. Through this interesting forum, she has encountered like-minded people with whom she feels great affinity. She has a particular interest in John and it seems that the friendship is progressing onto a more serious level.

Ellen's dream

'I saw myself with my sister and I was carrying a birthday cake. I think I could hear Joss Stone playing as well. The cake seemed to have been made of jelly and it was green. We walked and walked and then I was on my own and I saw myself in front of a building. It was really beautiful and I wanted to get into it somehow. There seemed to be different shops and offices inside, but everything was designer and I could see names like Chanel and Christian Dior. As I tried to walk in, a stern, threatening looking man stopped me and said that I wasn't good enough to enter the building. I felt upset and continued on my way. Then I got to a spiritualist church and I walked in. I felt so happy and serene there. Next there was a man who was really good to me. I remembered I still had the cake and I think we ate some of it. Later I was walking back towards the building. I just wanted to get in somehow. I noticed a door at the back. It was bright yellow and it was open, so I walked through. Then it was really strange, as the back door and the front door became one and the same.'

Analysis

Ellen's dream may be divided into two parts. The first section is an assessment of the past and the present in terms of goals, achievements and obstacles. The second part explores relevant future possibilities and offers constructive advice.

Part 1

'I saw myself with my sister and I was carrying a birthday cake. I think I could hear Joss Stone playing as well. The cake seemed to have been made of jelly and it was green. We walked and walked and then I was on my own and I saw myself in front of a building. It was really beautiful and I wanted to get into it somehow. There seemed to be different shops and offices inside, but everything was designer and I could see names like Chanel and Christian Dior. As I tried to walk in, a stern, threatening looking man stopped me and said that I wasn't good enough to enter the building. I felt upset and continued on my way.'

Ellen starts her dream with her sister and a birthday cake.

Birthday = an emphasis on significant times and events, particularly in relation to childhood influences.
Cake = celebration; emotional contentment.
Sister = representative of close female ties and relations.
Music = any piece of music that is pleasant and in tune points to emotional serenity and spiritual awareness; should the music prove harsh and offensive, a closer inspection of values and principals is recommended.
Musical instruments refer to personal hopes and preferences.

Ellen's sister is representative of a positive female influence which may well be an actual sister or alternatively this could point to a woman who shares similar characteristics with the sister portrayed in the dream. At times an individual could also be incorporated into a dream to depict a collective and in this particular case, it is possible that the sister is an overall symbolic assessment of all significant females in Ellen's life. The presence of the birthday cake emphasises further the importance of these women in terms of emotional contribution. The general overview so far points to close female relationships that probably go back to Ellen's childhood and whose effect have been of major importance in terms of support and emotional serenity.

Next, Ellen is aware of music by Joss Stone. The presence of 'Joss Stone' is primarily a play on words, provoked by her recent interest in psychic and spiritual development. Ellen has been burning 'joss sticks' quite regularly while meditating. The subconscious has included this association in order to emphasise the importance of these spiritual stirrings. This is confirmed further with the integration of music as its connotations are also affiliated with emotional wellbeing and spirituality. The fact that Ellen hears the music at this particular point in the dream suggests that her interest in this area could have started in childhood, although it seems that she had

never previously delved into it too deeply. Ellen is then aware that the cake is made from jelly and that it is green.

Jelly = participation in fun and simple activities can prove beneficial.
Green = refers to money matters, in particular financial transactions.

Since the cake is representative of emotional happiness and enjoyment, the fact that it is made of jelly and green suggests that perhaps Ellen's recent thoughts on fun and wellbeing have also included an assessment of financial issues.

After having walked for a period of time, Ellen finds herself on her own, in front of a beautiful building.

Walk = represents pace and movement through events and situations.
Alone = to enjoy being alone points to a need for peace and tranquillity;
to be left alone by force or to feel lonely indicates emotional upheaval.
Beauty = to be aware of beauty in a dream may be construed as extremely
positive as it indicates great joy and fulfilment.
Building = relates to goals and objectives.

This is a reference to Ellen's aims and ambitions. The overall suggestion is that success has not come to her easily or quickly as there seems to be a prolonged period of walking in the dream. Nevertheless, there is a strong indication of achievement and contentment in relation to career matters and a sense of peace as regards decisions. When Ellen finds herself alone in the dream, the accompanying feelings do not include dismay or loneliness. Furthermore, she seems to be exploring her options, looking for ways of achieving fulfilment and satisfaction. This is very much highlighted by the awareness of beauty in conjunction to the building.

Next Ellen notices the contents of the building and is overwhelmed by a desire to get in. Unfortunately, she does not manage to accomplish this task and is left feeling upset as she continues on her way.

Shop = represents choices and options as regards a particular situation.
Office = career-related decisions.
Man = represents masculine influences.
Threat = to feel threatened in a dream is an indication of unexpected
setbacks and competition accompanied by devious, underhanded dealings;
to threaten someone warns against poor judgement that can have serious
consequences.
Upset = an indication of disruption and upheaval.

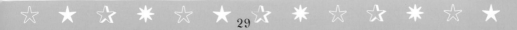

Initially as Ellen is looking into the building, her attention is drawn to the various shops and offices and seems quite taken by the fact that they are all designer. Given the fact that Ellen works as an interior designer, the association may be regarded as a reference to her hopes and aspirations. On one level, she is weighing up her options within the design industry, looking for a way forward, but on another level, the presence of designer names points to a wish to achieve prestige and status within the industry. However, there is a warning that this cannot be readily achieved since in the dream she does not initially manage to enter the building. There is strong competition associated with her line of work and some of the tactics employed by the opposition may be considered devious and questionable. There is also a suggestion that the problematic rivals are primarily men as it is a man who blocks her entry.

To some degree, perhaps Ellen blames herself as far as her current situation is concerned, since in the dream the man informs her that she is not good enough to enter the building. This appears to contradict how she has perceived her ability and achievement so far. Perhaps the longevity involved in fulfilling her highest aspirations has caused her inner frustration which although not always apparent, does lurk under the surface. This is emphasised further by the fact that she is left feeling upset pointing to disruptions and uncertainty. Nevertheless, in the dream she does manage to continue on her way which shows that her sense of purpose is very much intact and not marred by occasional feelings of insecurity.

Part 2

'Then I got to a spiritualist church and I walked in. I felt so happy and serene there. Next there was a man who was really good to me. I remembered I still had the cake and I think we ate some of it. Later I was walking back towards the building. I just wanted to get in somehow. I noticed a door at the back. It was bright yellow and it seemed open, so I walked through. Then it was really strange, as the back door and the front door became one and the same.'

As the dream progresses, there is a change of scenery. Ellen finds herself in a spiritualist church where she finds happiness and meets a man. Once again the cake comes into play.

Church = spiritual awakening.
Happy = an exceedingly positive omen, depicting triumph and pleasure.
Eat = any form of eating relates to desire and sexual energy.

Ellen's arrival at the church highlights her interest in spiritual matters. The fact that it is a spiritualist church simply emphasises the importance of the word 'spiritual'. This could be on more than one level, as the subconscious attempts to explore the potential of spiritual connotation in relation to Ellen's life. Here, she feels happy which is in stark contrast to what she experienced earlier on in the dream. Perhaps this is a clue, aimed at uncovering the true values and principles that would induce happiness in Ellen's life.

The arrival of the man is also of great significance, since it is at this point that Ellen remembers the cake once more. This may be regarded as an attempt to explore the opportunities that have now arisen with the existence of new encounters. The fact that they both decide to eat some of the cake refers to desire and sexual awakening within the relationship. As the symbolic meaning of the cake carries optimistic undertones, it may be assumed that there is potential in this situation for a serious involvement. This is reinforced with the inclusion of other positive symbols which interpreted together denote great harmony and balance between the spiritual and the physical.

Another interesting point about this new man is that Ellen feels he is very good to her. Perhaps this is a reflection of what she needs at the moment. She has endured much disappointment with a certain man in relation to her career. It seems that at least where her love life is concerned, she is hoping for honesty and devotion.

Next, Ellen feels an urge to go back to the building, still burning with the same desire to get in. Having failed at the front door, she finally succeeds using a back door. Once inside the building, however, she discovers that there is no difference between the two doors.

**Door = important new opportunities that can lead to significant changes.
Yellow = an optimistic outlook.**

The imagery of the doors is used as a reference to the arrival of fresh opportunities. Since Ellen does not seem to be able to enter through the front door, there is a suggestion that the more usual avenues associated with career advancement in her field will not prove effective. However, alternative routes may prove highly beneficial, as implied by the integration of an open back door. Its colour provides further confirmation of this idea, as yellow represents optimism and hope.

Once inside the building, Ellen feels that the two doors become one. This accentuates the fact that although her chosen option is not necessarily the correct route towards success, an alternative course will eventually achieve the desired effect.

Conclusion

Within this dream, Ellen's subconscious has explored her hopes and fears with an emphasis on potential outcome and consequence. As far as her career is concerned, presently there seems to be a lack of insight into her true needs. Although there is no objection to her ambitions, Ellen's ideas as to what this would actually entail are not in accordance to what her subconscious considers appropriate. For example, in the dream she seems exceptionally impressed with the various designer brands and then is besieged by a fear of inadequacy. Here, the subconscious does not agree with Ellen's analogy of what would be right for her and furthermore, it does not see her as incompetent. She is being told emphatically that her desire to become an established and renowned designer can be achieved, but the process should not take place for the sake of misguided, superficial ideologies. Her gifts and talents are in full effect and the recommendation is to choose a path that explores her natural abilities to their maximum potential. This would allow Ellen to shine naturally within an intensely competitive market and ultimately she should attain the kind of respect and prestige that she yearns for and deserves.

On an emotional level, Ellen's realisation of true happiness seems to be dependent on a lifestyle that is inspired and driven by sound spiritual beliefs. Furthermore, the application of these principles has proved exceptionally beneficial in terms of forming a solid foundation for a serious relationship.

Overall, this dream can be regarded as a careful examination of Ellen's true path to happiness as she embarks upon an important journey of self discovery and exploration.

EXAMPLE C:
An examination of traits and patterns
Subject: Heather

Background information: The recent ending of an important relationship with Mick has provoked Heather into much thought and reflection. Mick is divorced and has a child. He had been with Heather for a while and the disintegration of their relationship was seemingly due to the various complications in his life. Although Heather's dream is primarily instigated by the separation from Mick, it also includes issues surrounding her relationship with an ex-boyfriend, Gary, with whom she had been involved with many years ago.

Heather's dream

'I had a dream about Mick last night. I dreamed that I was on a train with him and I asked him why he's been so distant with me recently. I asked him whether it was because he'd met someone else and he said that it was and that they'd fallen for each other instantly. I was really hurt in my dream and wanted to know more, but before I could ask him more about it he jumped off the train at the next station, while I begged him to stop and come back. Then another ex of mine came into the dream, Gary. I was chatting to him on the phone. I can't remember much about the conversation apart from the fact that we were having a really pleasant chat and then suddenly his end went silent. After a few seconds I asked him what was going on and he said that he was driving and had had to brake very suddenly or he would have crashed. I think all this has probably got something to do with my brain trying to fathom out why relationships with people I really like never seem to work out.'

Analysis

This dream may be divided into two parts. The first section deals with Mick and the second is dedicated to Gary. These particular characters have been chosen by the subconscious in an attempt to highlight and dissect certain familiar patterns.

Part 1

'I had a dream about Mick last night. I dreamed that I was on a train with him and I asked him why he's been so distant with me recently. I asked him whether it was because he'd met someone else and he said that it was and that they'd fallen for each other instantly. I was really hurt in my dream and wanted to know more, but before I could ask him more about it he jumped off the train at the next station, while I begged him to stop and come back.'

The dream begins with both Heather and Mick on the train and the need for Heather to question Mick about his recent behaviour.

Train = refers to an event of major significance.
Question = hidden, unresolved issues.

The presence of the train in the dream implies that Mick has been a significant relationship in Heather's life. It may be construed, however, that Heather's effect on Mick has proven equally important, since both individuals are featured on the train. Heather's need to question Mick highlights her frustration in relation to certain

unresolved issues and may be regarded as a clear attempt by the subconscious to sift through existing material in the hope of finding satisfactory answers. Heather feels that Mick has been distant recently which suggests that she is not actually convinced as to the validity of their intimacy. Her main fear revolves around the possibility of a rival.

Rival = denotes immense animosity and mistrust and a need to confront long-held insecurities.

This refers to inner feelings of anger and dismay induced by a struggle to understand the reasons behind the break-up. Heather seems to think that Mick and the other woman fell in love instantly. An obvious interpretation places the emphasis on a lack of stability although from an alternative perspective the underlying debate rests upon Heather's hidden views about herself. There is an implication, however, that on a conscious level no significant exploration of the subject has been made so far; yet as Heather begs Mick not to leave the train, she proves her awareness of the challenges ahead.

Beg = an indication of major challenges, particularly within relationships. Station = points to an important and fateful period in time.

This indicates that she is now ready to tackle any pending emotional agenda and the fact that Mick actually gets off at the next station emphasises further the importance of this relationship as it becomes a catalyst and sets into motion a chain of thoughts and events that can ultimately change Heather's life.

As always, a vital consideration in conjunction to any given segment of a dream is the emotional content.

Hurt = any form of physical injury depicts disappointment and anguish; feeling emotionally hurt points to betrayal and deception.

In this particular case, Heather is left feeling hurt and rejected. This reveals a strong fear of treachery and deceit which stems from the existence of deep-rooted anxieties.

Part 2

'Then another ex of mine came into the dream, Gary. I was chatting to him on the phone. I can't remember much about the conversation apart from the fact that we

were having a really pleasant chat and then suddenly his end went silent. After a few seconds I asked him what was going on and he said that he was driving and had had to brake very suddenly or he would have crashed. I think all this has probably got something to do with my brain trying to fathom out why relationships with people I really like never seem to work out.'

Gary's arrival on the scene is initially rather pleasant and accompanied by a mood that feels comfortable and light-hearted. The conversation takes place over the telephone and although Heather can't remember much detail, the overall feeling at this point is one of contentment. There is an abrupt change, however, when Gary stops talking.

Talk = communication issues.
Telephone = refers to encounters and meetings.
Pleasant = to find something pleasant signifies an interesting and agreeable interlude.
Silence = to be aware of silence within a situation refers to a period of thought and reflection followed by major decisions.
Brake = caution against hasty decisions.
Collision = fear of losing control; impetuous, impulsive behaviour.

Since the use of the telephone may be interpreted as relevant encounters between Heather and Gary, the conversation that takes place is indicative of the type of contact and dialogue that may have initially existed in their relationship. The fact that Heather cannot remember much of what was said insinuates that perhaps not every moment was filled with excitement and vigour; nevertheless, during the early part of the affair there was a sense of peace and contentment and as this has been strongly featured in the dream, its importance should not be ignored.

Next, there is the question of Gary's silence and his subsequent explanation. It is interesting to note that as with the situation involving Mick, Heather needs to delve once more into the reasons behind what she perceives to be problematic behaviour. In effect, this section relates primarily to Gary's thoughts and feelings as observed and understood by Heather's subconscious. His silence signifies a period of reflection and it can be assumed that at some point he had started to explore the possibilities within the relationship. His initial objective had been to analyse its relevance in terms of future connotations, as illustrated by the act of driving.

Drive = represents progression through life.

However, in the dream he is besieged by a need to brake and a fear of collision which implies that regardless of surface appearances he had remained rather doubtful as regards to long-term prospects.

Brake = caution against hasty decisions.
Collision = fear of losing control; impetuous, impulsive behaviour.

It must be noted that this is not an indication of Gary's depth of feeling for Heather. From an emotional standpoint his motives had remained sincere as demonstrated by the need to examine likely scenarios. Furthermore, since there is no symbolic reference to an ending or any suggestion of underhanded behaviour, it may be assumed that Gary's intentions had been genuine.

Conclusion

This dream may be primarily regarded as an emotional dissection of Heather's love life. The separation from Mick has instigated a chain of associated questions and quandaries which should be understood, addressed and dealt with appropriately. In order to assist and accelerate this process, the subconscious has incorporated Gary into the equation. This has been through careful selection for the purpose of highlighting relevant similarities. The dream does not delve into the excuses or supposed reasons that were forwarded as justification for ending either relationship. Instead, it prompts an investigation of the common denominator, both in terms of Heather's attraction for these men and perhaps more importantly, in relation to the intrinsic motives for any subsequent separation. The key lies with an understanding of traits and patterns and a release from redundant, superfluous ideals and conditioning.

Heather's final comment as she recounts her dream is quite revealing:
'I think all this has probably got something to do with my brain trying to fathom out why relationships with people I really like never seem to work out.'

The subconscious of course, is already in possession of all the facts, but it is Heather's acknowledgement of these issues that will ultimately clarify the truth.

Recurring dreams

The aim of recurring dreams is to bring about acknowledgement and awareness by repeatedly replaying a particular set of images. Cases of recurring dreams have been known to appear intermittently over a number of years suggesting that until the conscious mind fully understands and deals with specific difficulties, the subconscious cannot abandon its quest for comprehension. Quite often recurring dreams point to severe anxieties and hidden feelings that can no longer remain dormant lest they lead to further setbacks. The following examples concentrate on the most common causes of recurring dreams.

EXAMPLE A:
Childhood-related issues

Subject: Paul

Background information: Paul is in his late twenties, studying at university and hoping to become a teacher. His father had hoped that Paul would stay within the realms of family tradition and study medicine. Although the relationship between Paul and his father has always been unstable, in recent years their disagreements have escalated out of control. Currently, Paul and his father barely communicate.

Paul's dream

'I started having this dream about a year ago. It always begins with someone tickling me. I can never see who the person is; I just know that I'm being tickled. Then I'm reading a newspaper and I'm approached by a king. I always nod when I see him. Then I don't know why but he has a sword and I suddenly have my own armour. I rebel against whatever it is that he's saying, although again, I don't know what it is that he says. I spit in his direction, wanting to offend him. Next, I see myself on the roof and there's a nest with a rabbit in it. I think this is a bird's nest and then I start wondering why there is a rabbit. I look at my nails. They look awful; it's as if I've been doing something with the nest. When I look at the nest again it's square, although I'm not sure how that's happened and then I wake up...'

Analysis

This dream may be divided into two sections. The first part dissects Paul's impressions of his father and explores the dynamics of their relationship. The second section concentrates on the need for emotional liberation.

Part 1

'It always begins with someone tickling me. I can never see who the person is; I just know that I'm being tickled. Then I'm reading a newspaper and I'm approached by a king. I always nod when I see him. Then I don't know why but he has a sword and I suddenly have my own armour. I rebel against whatever it is that he's saying, although again, I don't know what it is that he says. I spit in his direction, wanting to offend him.'

This dream begins with a reference to childhood.

Tickle = childhood pleasures.

Although Paul cannot see who is tickling him, he is very much aware of the action itself. This is a reminder of pleasant experiences that would have derived from different sources and as such their importance in relation to childhood memories should not be ignored. The fact that the dream initiates from a childhood perspective also implies that the root of all relevant anxieties would have originated during this period.

Next, Paul is approached by a king whilst reading a newspaper and is very much aware that he always nods upon the king's arrival.

Read = an indication of longing for greater knowledge, usually with an emphasis on a particular subject matter.
Newspaper = searching for the truth.
King = power; figure of authority.
Nod = seeking praise and approval.

The king represents Paul's father and the inclusion of this particular image suggests that from an early age, Paul's understanding of their relationship revolved around his father's projection of power and authority. The reference to reading a newspaper depicts Paul's attempts to have understood his father better and the consistent nodding highlights a frantic need to have gained his father's approval.

Here the tone of the dream changes. The emphasis shifts to the king's

threatening behaviour with a sword, leading to Paul's retaliation with armour accompanied by overtures of indignation and self defence.

Sword = a sign of power and ambition.
Armour = fears of inadequacy.
Rebel = a conflict of opinion.
Spit = contempt; disgust.
Offend = to be offended is a sign of harsh, inhospitable conditions in relation to social matters; to offend someone denotes anger and resentment within a relationship.

The presence of the sword reiterates Paul's impressions of his father in terms of power. This time, however, he is suddenly aware of his own armour which suggests that eventually he was overwhelmed with fears of inadequacy as he could not always manage to fulfil his father's expectations. This led to a period of conflict and gradually progressed to far more extreme feelings of resentment.

Part 2

'Next, I see myself on the roof and there's a nest with a rabbit in it. I think this is a bird's nest and then I start wondering why there is a rabbit. I look at my nails. They look awful; it's as if I've been doing something with the nest. When I look at the nest again it's square, although I'm not sure how that's happened and then I wake up...'

As Paul finds himself on the roof, he reveals that so far he has tried to remain cocooned and protected from the negative effects of the feelings provoked by his father. However, there is also an indication of misplaced fear as represented by the presence of the rabbit in the bird's nest.

Roof = feelings of self-preservation.
Nest = conditions are ready for change and development.
Rabbit = an indication of dread and fear.
Bird = generally in dreams birds represent hopes and aspirations.

Paul is aware that the rabbit does not belong in this setting. The nest highlights a time for progression and the emphasis on the type of nest points to hopes and aspirations that are now ready to be set into motion; but then Paul notices his nails and although his initial reaction is an awareness of their unsightliness, the

underlying factor lies with his bafflement as to how his nails reached that state.

Nail = on fingers and toes, nails relate to the finishing touches; should they appear clean or neatly polished, this would indicate a positive outcome where every detail has been considered with tremendous care and deliberation. If the nails appear unsightly, the suggestion would be one of persistent difficulties due to neglect. A nail being hammered into a wall refers to changes on the home front.

At this point the focus remains with the consequences of Paul's neglect of the real issues in question. The ultimate desire is to create safety and emotional assurance as suggested by the new shape of the nest.

Square = a desire for safety and security.

However, as demonstrated throughout the dream, such an immense objective cannot be achieved by disregarding deeply embedded and unresolved emotional antagonism.

Conclusion

In an attempt to lead a normal life, Paul has hidden and swept aside all feelings of anger and resentment towards his father. Although painful memories and emotions can be temporarily boxed and filed into the archives of the mind, they will eventually resurface causing setbacks and disruptions. As an adult, Paul's attempt at self-preservation has been to avoid controversy with his father and although this may have allowed him to function peacefully for a time, he cannot progress further or fulfil his hopes and ambitions without confronting the crux of the matter. The fact that he is continuously prompted by fear hinders his development suggesting that ultimately any future success and happiness will be dependent on a conclusive resolution of negative effects caused by the relationship with his father.

All through the dream there is a distinct sense of bewilderment as Paul questions the reasons behind certain unexpected scenarios; he has no real answers, only reactions to what he perceives as unusual peculiarities. This method of analysis seems to be a reflection of how he functions within the conscious domain. The subconscious however, yearns for a strategy to tackle problems with an astute sense of observation and acknowledgement, rather than doubt and evasion.

EXAMPLE B:
Trauma

Subject: Samantha

Background information: Samantha is in her late teens and from childhood has periodically suffered from bouts of depression. Her parents recently divorced and although this was inevitable, the ordeal has proved traumatic for Samantha, leaving her feeling hurt and vulnerable.

Samantha's dream

'I've dreamed this dream practically every night for the past few weeks. It's Easter, but we have a Christmas tree in the room. The tree looks sort of broken and wrong. I look at the TV and there's a programme about an elf. I pick up a camera and start taking photos. Then I see my Mum and hear the kettle at the same time. She's got some scissors in her hands. I kiss her on the cheek. She says something about my complexion not looking right. Then she looks at me and tells me that she has cancer. The electricity cuts off at that point. I just feel as if I don't know anything; it's all a mystery to me. I start crying and I wake up...'

Analysis

This dream can be divided into two sections. The first part offers information on how Samantha views emotional interaction within the family. The second part focuses primarily on specific relations and Samantha's current impressions of her life and her future.

Part 1

'It's Easter, but we have a Christmas tree in the room. The tree looks sort of broken and wrong. I look at the TV and there's a programme on an elf. I pick up a camera and start taking photos.'

The dream starts with the presence of a Christmas tree despite the fact that it is Easter.

Easter = a yearning to replenish on all levels.
Christmas tree = a brightly lit and decorated Christmas tree refers to

unexpected family reunions. Should the tree appear mundane or damaged, there is a longing for closer family bonds.

The damaged appearance of the tree suggests family problems and a lack of unity. Samantha would like a closer bond between family members, believing that solidarity would improve their living conditions. This ideology may be a reflection of her experiences as indicated by the incorporation of the elf and the television.

Elf = childhood memories and experiences.
Television = depicts activity and movement in conjunction with new information.

It seems that periodically the presence of new conditions or advice has shifted the dynamics of the relationships within the family. Given Samantha's history of depression, this could even be a reference to temporary changes brought about by counselling and professional therapy. However, she has also realised that there are no long-term certainties, as demonstrated by the presence of the camera and the photographs.

Camera = deception; illusion.
Photograph = a review of past events and experiences.

Past advice may have initially emerged as successful, but a more extensive review of associated events points to a sense of illusion and temporary wellbeing.

Part 2

Then I see my Mum and hear the kettle at the same time. She's got some scissors in her hands. I kiss her on the cheek. She says something about my complexion not looking right. Then she looks at me and tells me that she has cancer. The electricity cuts off at that point. I just feel as if I don't know anything; it's all a mystery to me. I start crying and I wake up...'

Samantha's mother not only represents herself in the dream but also touches on other connected issues.

Mother = nurturing instincts.
Kettle = domestic comfort and wellbeing.

Her mother's appearance occurs simultaneously with the sound of the kettle, implying that Samantha's vision of domestic wellbeing relies on the mother figure. This also correlates with the underlying symbolic significance of the mother, further emphasising the importance of this relationship in connection to Samantha's ideas of comfort and security. Next, she is aware that her mother is holding a pair of scissors.

Scissors = a decision whether to end or remould an existing relationship.

The presence of the scissors refers to her parents' marriage and the gradual build-up to the divorce. Clearly, the decision was not taken lightly and as it is Samantha's mother who is in possession of the scissors, it can be assumed that it was indeed her decision to ultimately push forward the divorce. Samantha now kisses her mother on the cheek.

Kiss = a desire to love; a longing to share and express emotion.
Cheek = refers to emotional issues.

Again, emotions are at the forefront of this dream. There is an implication of persistent emotional problems and Samantha longs to express her true feelings in an open way. This is further reiterated by her mother's comments about Samantha's complexion.

Complexion = a clear complexion denotes health and happiness; complexion that appears ill or disfigured relates to emotional instability and problematic health issues.

This may be a statement about Samantha's periodic spells of depression. Her mother's next comment touches on the feelings of both women on this issue.

Cancer = to have cancer refers to unresolved problems that are directly and constantly affecting everyday life. To see a person with cancer suggests worry and guilt caused by the inability to face one's fears.

Samantha's mother informs her that she has cancer. In this case, the feelings of guilt and insecurity associated with this symbol may relate to either woman. Samantha feels guilty because she believes her illness contributed to her parents' divorce; her mother's guilt is due to an awareness of the consequences of her actions, acknowledging the fact that her decision to divorce has proved detrimental to

her daughter's health. Next the electricity cuts out.

Electricity = optimism; light at the end of the tunnel.

Although the disappearance of electricity at this point relates to feelings of pessimism and despair, Samantha is then aware of a sense of mystery.

Mystery = an indication of hidden blessings.

Regardless of Samantha's feelings of helplessness, the interpretation associated with mystery still reassures and reaffirms the presence of light at the end of the tunnel. However, the fact remains that Samantha always cries before waking up.

Cry = frustration; helplessness.

This indicates that the process of recovery will require time and will inevitably prove difficult and painful.

Conclusion

For Samantha, her parents' divorce has proved traumatic and this has led to an attempt by the subconscious to analyse her perception of the situation. The fact that the dream is a recurring one highlights a desperate need to resolve feelings of guilt and helplessness. The greater message being conveyed is that current conditions are not beyond hope and despite gloomy appearances, the possibility of unexpected blessings should not be ignored.

EXAMPLE C:
Hidden Memory

Subject: Jack

Background information: Jack is in his mid twenties. When he was fourteen years old, he witnessed a robbery at a post office while on holiday in Spain. At the time he could only recall minor details of the incident as he had managed to hide behind a counter and his line of vision had been limited. However, it is also believed that he was in shock and as a result blocked out much of what he could have seen. For the first time since, Jack recently returned to Spain and although the trip was to a different area, it nevertheless triggered a recurring dream.

Jack's dream

'I see myself hiding in a cupboard. Through a crack I can see what's going on outside. There are three men in sandals. But the sandals are also skates and they're skating everywhere. I can hear music. It sounds terrible and then two of them start singing a duet which sounds just as bad. Then they seem to be trying to strangle each other and I always think at this point that I'm supposed to notice something. Then one of them sort of becomes a part of the furniture or the walls of the post office or something and all I know is that what I'm seeing is very wrong and then I wake up.'

Analysis

There is no need to divide this dream into segments as it may be considered a brief, yet highly informative account of a specific set of events designed purely for the purpose of divulging factual material.

Jack begins by seeing himself hiding in a cupboard.

Hide = fear of exposure; weakness and vulnerability.
Cupboard = order and organisation can help eliminate current difficulties.

On one level, this is a reference to Jack's original ordeal. He was hiding at the time of the robbery and he would have been afraid of exposure but from a symbolic perspective the fact that he's blocked out the incident can also point to feelings of weakness and vulnerability. The presence of the cupboard, however, suggests that the events of that particular day can be remembered and resolved through a methodical approach. Next, Jack sees three men in sandals, although the sandals also appeared to be skates.

Sandals = relates to financial issues and in particular highlights conditions that require greater flexibility and liberation from a monetary perspective.
Skate = an indication of rapid movement and progression.

An extremely interesting point is that according to sources at the time there were only two thieves present in the post office. As this is a recurring dream based on a memory relating to actual events, the presence of three men in the dream should be considered carefully. The sandals relate to the motive for the robbery, which is clearly financial gain and the reference to the skates suggests that the events relating to the robbery took place with speed and precision.

Next the emphasis lies with music and singing.

Music = a piece of music that is pleasant and in tune points to emotional serenity and spiritual awareness; should the music prove harsh and offensive, a closer inspection of values and principals is recommended. Musical instruments refer to personal hopes and preferences.
Sing = should the singing be in tune, it denotes a satisfactory outcome to an emotional decision; singing that is out of tune or unpleasant is a sign of emotional uncertainty and dilemma.
Duet = loyal friends.

As two of the men attempt a duet, it may be assumed that they know each other very well. However, the third man is not included in the singing, insinuating that his involvement is possibly based on different circumstances. Jack is aware that the music sounds harsh and the singing is out of tune. This implies that at the time of the robbery uncertainty in the robbers' demeanour or interaction with each other was noted by Jack's subconscious.

Then the men try to strangle each other and Jack thinks he should be now noticing something important.

Strangle = to be strangled denotes resentment and anger towards a situation that has been based on power play and intimidation; to strangle someone, warns against thoughtless and hasty behaviour that can prove regretful; to watch someone being strangled recommends a closer look at surrounding relationships where there may be uncomfortable questions as regards conduct and demeanour.

The clue lies with a closer inspection of a relationship that seems to operate on the outside. Already, there has been a suggestion that the facts surrounding one of the men may be different to the other two and this is now highlighted further with the symbolic meaning of watching someone being strangled. There is also an indication of questionable conduct. While on one level this can relate to the unacceptable act of robbery, from another perspective there may be a suggestion that this is not usual behaviour for these men.

Next, Jack sees one of the men blend into the structure of the post office and become a part of it. This hints at a connection between one of the thieves and the post office. A likely scenario is that he is perhaps an employee which could then offer an explanation as to why all the way through the dream one of the men has been singled out. The link between the thief and the post office can also relate

to Jack's final comment on the dream, stating that as the man merges into the building, Jack feels that there is something very wrong. A disloyal, criminal employee could certainly induce such a reaction.

Conclusion

Jack's return to Spain triggered a probing of associative memories that had remained dormant for a number of years. The bulk of the information had been attained subconsciously, although due to the traumatic nature of the robbery it proved impossible for any details to emerge at the time. Nevertheless this is an excellent example of how the subconscious can gather relevant material under most circumstances. Perhaps even more intriguing is the fact that the information does not get lost or distorted, but merely stored until the conditions are suitable for further evaluation and analysis. Quite often, recurring dreams containing hidden memory will only stop when the information has been fully acknowledged and understood.

Dreams prompted by physical and environmental conditions

In this type of dream, a sequence of images is incorporated into the main format as a result of overwhelming external conditions. It is possible for a dream to be based entirely on environmental influences, although more commonly the dream is created within the parameters of one of the other dream categories and is then modified to accommodate unexpected developments. For instance, a dream may begin its projection as psychological but is then altered as irregularities in external conditions affect its natural flow. At times, it is possible to determine at which point in the dream the interruption takes place. In such a situation, the unaffected part of the dream may still be interpreted accordingly, while images induced by physical and environmental conditions can be discarded.

When in doubt as to an exact moment of change, it would be unwise to take the dream too seriously as very little significance can be attached to the imagery.

For instance, should a dream be manipulated by indigestion, there would be limited symbolic definition relating to the precise point of change. The irregularities contained within such cases can cause ambiguity and speculation in respect to the nature of the imagery and therefore can never be regarded as conclusive. The following example relates to the most common type of dreams in this category.

EXAMPLE A:
Partial definition

Subject: Anthony
Background information: Anthony is eighteen years old and has been revising heavily for his exams. He has been very worried and overwhelmed by the ordeal.

Anthony's dream

'I dreamed I was trying to climb a hill and it was so hard and I just didn't know if I would ever reach the top. Suddenly the wind started to blow and all around me there was snow and ice. I was trying to walk, but my feet felt wet and numb and I started shivering and then I woke up…'

Analysis

The dream begins with Anthony's attempt at climbing a hill.

Climb = trials and tribulations.
Hill = setbacks.

This is a reference to Anthony's exams. In the dream, he finds the act of climbing difficult and feels uncertain about reaching the top. In reality, Anthony feels nervous about his exams and feels unsure about the outcome.

The remainder of the dream, however, has been manipulated by external elements. The following is an account of what Anthony noticed upon waking up:

'When I woke up, it was raining really hard and the wind had flung open the window. The temperature in my room had completely dropped. Since my bed is right under the window, the sheets had got wet and my feet were soaked.'

In this dream, the imagery used to portray cold and damp has been inspired by

environmental conditions. The subconscious has become distracted by changes in physical circumstances and has altered the natural sequence of the dream to convey the new developments.

Conclusion

Anthony's dream has been modified to include additional material relevant to changes in external conditions. Clearly, even with this style of dream, the subconscious still attempts to relay information. However, the substance of the facts in question is normally based upon brief physical influences which although appropriate at that moment in time, serve no other significant function.

Predictive dreams

The most captivating aspect of this type of dream is that it is considered a vision of actual events and experiences. As the prophetic information contained within these dreams cannot be easily defined or explained, there remains persistent speculation in connection to the mechanical workings of the subconscious. Questions concerning the source and origin of such amazing knowledge have continued throughout history and although various attempts have been made at producing a feasible explanation, no definitive answers have yet been presented. Nevertheless, the fascination with this subject continues and despite the lack of evidence in terms of method and procedure, the mere existence of such incredible dreams reaffirms the boundless capacity of the subconscious.

The following examples highlight the most common types of predictive dream. The usual symbolic interpretation that is applied to other genres of dream is rarely applicable here, as predictive dreams operate primarily outside the realms of psychologically induced imagery. The first example may be considered an exact narrative of actual events, accurately projected to the last detail. The second example contains some symbolic reference. The application of the imagery however, is not completely restricted to the usual format and this must be taken into consideration in order to attain optimum results.

EXAMPLE A:

Prophetic narrative

Subject: Andrea

Background information: Andrea's heightened perception and unusual psychic ability has allowed her access to a range of extraordinary phenomena. This particular dream relates to the circumstances around her father's death. About a year ago, Andrea's father was found dead in Paris. The events surrounding his death had appeared mysterious at the time, as no one had been informed he was going on a trip. The week prior to his death, Andrea had been excessively worried and on the occasions that she had managed to contact her father, he had reassured her that all was well. However, Andrea had remained unconvinced, sensing secrets and pending danger. This dream occurred on the very night her father died and may be considered a chronicle of the events leading to his death.

Andrea's dream

'I saw my father in Paris. I felt that he knew the place very well and that puzzled me, since in all these years he had not once mentioned being there. He was nervous as he got into a taxi. He gave the driver a piece of paper with an address on it and as the taxi set off, he reached into his briefcase and took out a letter and started reading it. I knew he had read that letter several times. I could see what was written. It was all to do with a woman my father had had an affair with seventeen years ago. She was informing him of a child that she had never told him about. She had been pregnant when my father ended the affair. Although I was shocked at the revelation of this affair and all that it represented, I was even more aware of my father's sense of desperation and confusion. He was riddled with feelings of guilt, both in relation to us, his true family and for that other woman and the unknown child. A part of him was outraged that she never told him something so important; but then he started thinking about what he would have done if she had told him. He just didn't know. I could see the woman's name at the end of the letter; she was called Emily. The reason Emily had written to my father after all these years was because her daughter, Veronica, had inadvertently come across photos, letters and documentations relating to her true identity. Veronica had not been aware that the man she had called her father all these years had not been her biological parent. Emily had met an American working in Paris while still pregnant with my father's child and married him soon after the baby was born. Her husband had assumed the role of the father in the child's life. According to Emily, Veronica

still considered the man that raised her as her true dad but was determined to meet the man who was her natural father. She had threatened to find him herself, if no one helped in the matter.

My father's eyes were filled with tears. I don't think I had ever seen him so upset. I knew then that he was on his way to meet the two women. At this point, I had an insight into what he had felt for Emily. He had loved her once; maybe not as much as he loved my mother but I knew she had been important to him. My own heart was broken and I wanted to wake up, but I just couldn't. I had to see it through. As the taxi stopped at a traffic light, I noticed my father looking towards a street. This is where he used to meet Emily. There was a small apartment in a very large building and they used to see each other a few days every month. I realised then that he managed these trips to Paris while he was supposedly away on business. He had to go to Germany a lot, so a few days in Paris wouldn't have been that hard to arrange. I could feel my own disappointment as I finally understood my father's secret; but at the same time, I knew that I would love him no matter what he'd done and I wished there was some way I could help him.

He finally arrived at his destination. He approached the door and tried to ring the bell, but there was something wrong with it and he had to press it a few times before it worked. Then I saw him with Emily and Veronica. The women started to cry and so did I. I watched my father hold back the tears. He thought Emily hadn't changed much and that Veronica looked just like me. I looked at her and he was right. I don't know what was said, even though I was trying hard to focus on that scene. It's as if I wasn't allowed to see beyond that point. Next I saw my father in the taxi, heading back to the hotel, broken and distraught. My heart started hurting. I knew there was something wrong. As I saw him enter his room, I realised he was so engrossed in his emotional pain, he hadn't noticed any of the physical symptoms. I watched him have a heart attack and as I woke up sobbing, I knew my father was dead.'

Analysis

As all the events are actual and exact, there are no symbolic connotations. Following her father's death, Andrea went to Paris, retraced his movements as portrayed in her dream and found every detail to be remarkably accurate. Nevertheless, there are some points that even within the context of such extraordinary precision, remain open to suggestion and interpretation. The inclusion of the faulty bell, for instance, may be regarded as a puzzle. After all, its relevance to the subject matter may appear practically nominal. Whether Andrea actually sees the problem with the bell or is left oblivious to it does not add or detract from the general basis of the crucial events in the dream; but perhaps from an alternative perspective this piece of

information is vital. When Andrea finally decided to meet Emily and Veronica, all she could think about was the bell and whether it would prove faulty. Ultimately it did and with this particular knowledge she had her own personal sense of realisation as to the importance and accuracy of the facts that were revealed in relation to her father's secret relationship. This is a clear example of how the subconscious manages to incorporate details of personal concern and association, even within the domain of predictive dreams.

Another interesting point in this dream is that Andrea is not privy to the conversation that takes place between her father and the two women. A possible suggestion may be that her subconscious considered further involvement inappropriate at that time partly due to the emotionally painful nature of the discovery, but also because ultimately, Andrea would have to decide for herself whether or not to instigate further contact with Emily and Veronica.

Conclusion

Apart from informing Andrea of her father's tragic death, the dream serves to reveal hidden truths which needed to emerge. It is interesting that despite her unusually developed sense of intuition, Andrea had never previously sensed her father had had an affair. It must be remembered, however, that seventeen years ago she was a teenager and perhaps not quite ready to digest such disruptive revelations. Her subconscious, driven by a careful examination of all available data as well as a need for self-preservation, deliberated and waited until the conditions were ready for the truth to be revealed. Once again, this highlights the immense power of the subconscious, not only in connection to the accumulation of knowledge but also as regards the selective application of all relevant material.

EXAMPLE B:
Manipulated narrative

Subject: David

Background information: David is in his early thirties and single. His involvements with women, although mostly pleasant, have never actually proven serious or demanded much thought or reflection. It may be assumed that from an emotional perspective David has not so far been challenged in his views and principles. However, the following dream was prompted as a prelude to the arrival of unusual circumstances. Usually, David does not remember many details from his dreams, but when he does, the dreams tend to be of a predictive nature.

David's dream

'I had this dream a few days before my trip. In my dream, I was at a station and running to catch a train. I just managed to jump on but as I did, I dropped my suitcase. It was sitting on the platform as the train pulled away. I was furious. I tried not to think about it too much. I sat down and started thinking about where I was going. I was on my way to see my cousin. When I got there, she told me there was a film on TV she wanted to watch. Next there was someone at the door. It was a beautiful girl. She came in and started flirting with me. Her name was Lucy. My cousin said that the girl was married and that I should be careful. I didn't pay much attention. I couldn't help myself; I was just so attracted to this girl. She had beautiful long curly brown hair. I kept looking at it. I wanted to kiss her but I was scared something bad would happen if I did. Then it was just me and the girl in a place I'd never seen before. I really wanted her, but at the same time, I knew it would all go wrong if I did something. I looked at her and looked at the door and had to choose whether to stay or go…'

Analysis

Although this particular dream has been partially manipulated by the subconscious and certain symbolic references have been incorporated, the facts in the dream have an uncanny resemblance to the actual experience. In order to demonstrate this point, the following is an account of the real events that took place:

'I was running to catch a flight and even though I made it, once I got to my destination, I realised that my luggage hadn't. I was so annoyed. I tried to calm myself down and went looking for my cousin who I knew was somewhere in the airport waiting for me. I hadn't seen her a while, so we had a lot to catch up on. Later, she suggested going to the cinema. When we got back home, a friend of hers came by. She was stunning. I was mesmerised by her eyes. They were so big and brown and the way she was looking at me… I can't describe it. She was introduced as Lucy. After some chit chat, it came out that Lucy was living with someone, which got me worried a bit but it didn't really put me off. Maybe it's because she was sitting in front of me and still looking at me the way she did. I wanted to see her again the next day, but I was only going to be there a few days and there was no real opportunity. We swapped numbers and she left. When I got home the reality of the situation hit me. I could call her, but then where was it all going to go? Even if she finished with her boyfriend for me, how did I know that she wouldn't do the same thing to me one day? This was all new territory. I'd never bothered with an attached woman before. I wasn't sure what to do…'

Although the dream includes symbolic representation, this has not occurred solely for the purpose of deeper underlying analysis. The subconscious has primarily substituted one situation with a similar replacement without particularly changing, hiding or detracting from the original act. For example, in the dream David is late for the train and loses his suitcase. In reality, he's late for his flight and his luggage gets misplaced. Whether he catches a train or a plane is not of crucial significance, since the importance merely lies with the fact that he goes on a journey. However, in both scenarios David loses his luggage which suggests that although some imagery may be used as representation, the underlying message remains the same. As regards this particular example, the idea conveyed is simply that there is a trip and the luggage gets left behind.

Further in the dream, there is a reference to watching television. In reality, David and his cousin go to the cinema. Since the objective is to watch a film, the subconscious substitutes the cinema with television. This does not alter the actual theme of the events in question. On this occasion whether a film is viewed on television or in the setting of a cinema is not of major consequence and the relevance of incorporating the act of watching a film into the dream is essentially for the sake of continuity in relation to the sequence of actual events.

The reason for the formation of this dream is based upon the arrival of Lucy. The circumstances around the details produced in the dream are very similar to those experienced in reality. For instance, in the dream there is a suggestion that she is married. Her actual status is not married, but very much attached as it transpires that Lucy lives with her boyfriend. In the dream, David is attracted to Lucy's hair. In reality, he is mesmerised by her eyes. Both scenarios depict David's awareness of her physical attributes, with an emphasis on sexual undertones. In the dream the description applied to Lucy's hair suggests a beautiful feature that stands out. In reality, David's description implies the same thing about her eyes. Once more, the point being conveyed is not so much an analysis of the hair or the eyes, but rather an observation, highlighting feelings of immense physical attraction.

The ultimate dilemma lies with the decision whether or not to pursue the possibilities further. In the dream, David finds himself in an unknown place; in his actual account of the events, he mentions that he has never been in this position before. The symbolic reference is obvious and in this particular example, the correlation may just as easily be incorporated into other dream categories. This indicates that even within the style of a predictive dream, the presence of symbolic association in its various forms can occur alongside actual events. In the final scene of the dream, David looks at the door and must decide whether to stay or go. In his actual version, he weighs up his options, trying to decide whether or not to enter into an affair. Once again, the symbolic reference that has been applied would be

just as prevalent and appropriate in other types of dream. In terms of the message being conveyed, both in the dream and in actual fact David must choose his next move.

Conclusion

The basis of this dream lies primarily with the existence of an unknown factor in a given situation. The arrival of a woman who is attached proves problematic on many levels. It may be assumed that the intensity of the attraction together with the fear of pending disaster has led to the creation of a dream which does not in itself offer solutions but merely highlights the importance of this particular situation. It should also be remembered that David had this dream a few days prior to the events taking place. This seems like an effort on the part of the subconscious to prepare him for this fatalistic encounter, by encouraging him to consider the pitfalls and theoretically deliberate upon his options should such conditions arise. Perhaps this way, the emotional effect of the events may prove slightly more controlled, enabling David to make a decision based on an analytical exploration of the possible outcome, as well as the unavoidable influence of desire and attraction.

Nightmares

Nightmares are usually produced by the subconscious in relation to situations that may be out of control. Usually there is significant emotional bearing associated with the dream and the imagery incorporated may appear exaggerated or distressing. Nightmares are often formed when both conscious and subconscious attempts at addressing sensitive material have failed. This particular form of neglect stems from either a fear of confrontation or the denial of a problem.

Most nightmares seem to occur within the psychological or recurring dream categories. It should also be pointed out that a nightmare is a very personal experience with its roots set within the psyche of the subject. These peculiarities can range from fears and phobias to specific childhood experiences. For instance, should the subject suffer from a phobia of spiders, a dream containing a spider would be recognised as a nightmare. The following examples relate to the psychological and recurring categories.

EXAMPLE A:
Psychological

Subject: Robert

Background information: Robert is in his forties and has suffered from a mild form of obsessive compulsive disorder from childhood. His obsession lies with cleanliness and order. His extraordinary neatness as a child was initially commended as an impressive attribute. With the passage of time, however, it became increasingly obvious that his behaviour was not merely based on a conscientious attempt at tidiness. Although he has had some professional help in relation to his problem, Robert feels that the solution will emerge through his own efforts. So far, the mild nature of this illness has allowed Robert to conceal his condition. Recently, he met Denise with whom a fairly close relationship has evolved. Robert has not yet discussed his condition with her and feels uncertain as to what his next move should be. The following dream has been induced by this current dilemma.

Robert's dream

'I picked up a pen and a piece of paper to write a letter to Denise. When I finished, I made my way to a barn where I thought she'd be. She was there. I could smell her perfume. It was lovely. Just for a second I felt so happy. She seemed to be holding some sheets, or linen or something. I could see the labels on them. Then I was naked. I looked at my arm. There was something moving on it. I just thought it was bacteria. Then it started spreading and I was covered with it. I started to run. I had to get to a bathroom somewhere. I was just running and running and I could feel the bacteria getting into my mouth. Then I felt my teeth loosen and fall out. I was just sick and dying. I called out Denise's name. I wanted her to help me.'

Analysis

This dream can be divided into two sections. The first part concentrates on the dynamics of the relationship with Denise, while the second highlights hopes and fears and makes further recommendations.

Part 1

'I picked up a pen and a piece of paper to write a letter to Denise. When I finished, I made my way to a barn where I thought she'd be. She was there. I could smell her

perfume. It was lovely. Just for a second I felt so happy. She seemed to be holding some sheets, or linen or something. I could see the labels on them.'

The dream begins with Robert's desire to write a letter.

Pen = signifies a more proactive attitude towards communication.
Paper = freedom of choice; decisions yet to be made.
Letter = to receive a letter signifies greater dialogue and communication; to write a letter recommends a more sincere and open approach as regards a particular situation.

Although no definite decision has yet been made, there is an indication that Robert feels ready to explore his options in terms of communication and discussion.
    Next, Robert is in a barn, where he thinks Denise would be.

Barn = an appreciation of simplicity; an unpretentious approach.

The image of the barn is incorporated in relation to Denise. This is perhaps an insight into Denise's character, emphasising a simple, down-to-earth attitude. There is also a suggestion that she would be approachable. Given Robert's doubts and fears as regards his condition, Denise's open and natural demeanour could prove highly comforting.
    Once in the barn with Denise, Robert is aware of her perfume and for just a moment, feels happy.

Smell = to be aware of a pleasant smell denotes joy and gratification; an offensive smell points to a potentially damaging situation.
Perfume = sensuality; attraction.
Happy = an exceedingly positive omen, depicting triumph and pleasure.

The symbolic references at this point depict pleasure and contentment. The perfume highlights Robert's attraction for Denise. As there is no negative imagery associated with her it may be assumed that Robert's subconscious sees Denise as a positive influence. He is worried, however, that any prospects of happiness would be short-lived. It may be assumed that Robert is afraid of the consequences of any revelations. Although he would like to tell Denise the truth, he also dreads possible rejection.
    Next, he notices the linen and the labels.

Linen = if the linen appears fresh and clean, honesty and openness in love is depicted; soiled linen points to lies, deceit and infidelity.
Label = it is important to look at the bigger picture and not dwell deeply on trivial details.

Since it is Denise who is holding the linen, it may be deduced that her feelings for Robert are completely genuine. The presence of the labels can be examined from two different perspectives; on one level they refer to Denise's attitude, suggesting that she would not allow minor details to affect her overall perception of the relationship. Alternatively, the labels represent Robert's disorder which can to an extent be interpreted as an obsession with trivia. Since Robert has always assumed that he would one day resolve his condition, perhaps the arrival of Denise in his life can give him the incentive that he needs to start the process.

Part 2

'Then I was naked. I looked at my arm. There was something moving on it. I just thought it was bacteria. Then it started spreading and I was covered with it. I started to run. I had to get to a bathroom somewhere. I was just running and running and I could feel the bacteria getting into my mouth. Then I felt my teeth loosen and fall out. I was just sick and dying. I called out Denise's name. I wanted her to help me.'

This section of the dream begins with Robert appearing naked.

Naked = to see oneself naked in a dream points to a fear of exposure; it also highlights growing emotional problems due to a lack of confidence; to see others naked implies that certain truths and realities are about to be revealed.

Once again, Robert's fears are at the forefront of the situation. Perhaps he sees his condition as a flaw and feels uncomfortable at the prospect of appearing weak and out of control.

At this point, some of the imagery included has been partially induced and formulated in conjunction with Robert's disorder. As his obsession revolves around hygiene and cleanliness, the integration of symbols such as bacteria is prompted mainly by fear and anxiety. Nevertheless, it should also be taken into consideration that this particular dream has come about in connection with decisions surrounding a relationship and as such a closer look at the symbolic connotations may still prove beneficial.

The initial appearance of bacteria occurs on the arm, but soon it spreads everywhere.

Arm = relates to personal relationships.
Bacteria = a warning not to allow trivial annoyances to escalate and develop into grossly exaggerated problems.

Although the presence of bacteria is predominantly instigated by the disorder, its symbolic meaning resonates with Robert's dilemma, warning him not to lose sight of what really matters. Since he first notices the bacteria on his arm, the emphasis lies with a need to protect the relationship.

Robert then starts to run and this seems to continue for a while.

Run = an indication of obstacles that need to be overcome.

The time is right for Robert both to confront his inner demons and also to tell Denise his secret. The urgency to find a bathroom in the dream further corroborates this issue.

Bathroom = depending on the other details seen in the dream, the bathroom can deal with a variety of issues; however, in all cases the emphasis remains with the need to cleanse and dispose of a particular situation in order to proceed to the next level.

In order for Robert to be able to enter a new phase, he must first confront current difficulties with a view to finding suitable solutions.

Robert is then aware of bacteria entering his mouth and he start losing his teeth.

The presence of the bacteria in the mouth signifies problems around expression and communication, particularly as regards the OCD. Since teeth generally relate to health matters, Robert's subconscious is referring to the disorder as an illness. Furthermore, the fact that Robert's teeth fall out in the dream, conveys a recommendation by the subconscious to seek medical advice.

Robert feels sick and dying at this point.

Sick = any form of sickness is a sign of emotional difficulties.
Die = a prominent sign of change; a desperate urge for emotional detachment in a highly charged situation.

The emotional difficulties associated with the situation are being highlighted. From

Robert's perspective, consulting a doctor may depict defeat, especially as he has insisted that he can combat the disorder on his own. His defiance could also be due to the existence of previous therapy and consultation that may have proved disappointing. Nevertheless, the subconscious continues to emphasise the importance of change and the need for a more detached and logical approach towards the illness.

Finally, Robert calls out Denise's name hoping for her assistance.

Name = any references to names in dreams highlight situations in conjunction to the people in question; to hear one's own name is a reminder to be more vigilant.
Help = to ask for help points to an awakening and a true understanding of what is required in order to accomplish and progress; to offer help suggests a need for greater emotional involvement.

Despite the painful undercurrent of the dream, Robert's desire to ask Denise for help may be regarded as a positive sign, suggesting that as far as this relationship is concerned, success is very much within reach, but is dependent upon a clear course of action.

Conclusion

After years of struggle with obsessive compulsive disorder, the arrival of Denise on the scene has triggered a need for a more decisive approach towards the situation. Robert's subconscious considers Denise a suitable candidate for long-term involvement and as such has attempted to prompt Robert into reflection and communication. The dream begins calmly and then turns into a nightmare, suggesting some urgency and pressure in relation to pending decisions. Ultimately what is being encouraged is a major evaluation of current attitudes and principles, together with an honest examination of fears and insecurities. For Robert to enjoy a new chapter in his life, he must first address those all too familiar demons.

EXAMPLE B:
Recurring

Subject: Laura

Background information: Laura is in her mid-fifties and after thirty years of marriage, has recently endured a traumatic separation. Her husband began an affair with a younger woman which prompted him to ask Laura for a divorce. Despite her anger and disbelief, she has secretly hoped for reconciliation, but has discovered much to her dismay, that her husband's intentions towards the new woman are serious. This has forced Laura to face the reality of her situation. Apart from emotional disappointment, there is much anxiety at the prospect of returning to work and frustration in relation to financial matters. Fear of social embarrassment also seems to be high on the agenda. It may be assumed that until recently, Laura had very little experience of such difficulties, having led a reasonably comfortable marriage with very few concerns.

Laura's dream

'I started having this dream soon after my husband left. It always begins with me knowing that I'm paralysed. I can sense danger everywhere. Then I see a vampire coming towards me. I try to move, but I can't. He stops and threatens me with all sorts and I try to get up and defend myself, but it's no use. Next thing I feel is pain and I start bleeding. There's so much blood. I remember I have a pill. I wonder to myself if I should take this pill now and as I do it tastes very, very bitter. Then I see myself in an office. I keep looking at my watch. I know I should be sorting my accounts, but I'm no good at maths. I keep thinking I have all these debts and someone's going to get me. I hear these whispers. I look at my clothes. They're still covered in blood. Next something feels different. There's no air. I see my husband. He's changed into a monster. I try to get up, but I can't. I'm still paralysed. I keep thinking there's no air. Then I think he's going to kill me. I'm choking. I wake up palpitating and covered in sweat...'

Analysis

This dream may be divided into two sections. The first part examines the emotional aspects of the situation, while the second looks at the broader implications of the divorce.

<h1 style="text-align:center">Part 1</h1>

'I started having this dream soon after my husband left. It always begins with me knowing that I'm paralysed. I can sense danger everywhere. Then I see a vampire coming towards me. I try to move, but I can't. He stops and threatens me with all sorts and I try to get up and defend myself, but it's no use. Next thing I feel is pain and I start bleeding. There's so much blood. I remember I have a pill. I wonder to myself if I should take this pill now and as I do it tastes very, very bitter.'

The dream begins with Laura's paralysis and her awareness of danger.

Paralysis = feeling trapped and hindered; restrictions.
Danger = signifies unrealistic expectations.

The paralysis represents thoughts and feelings induced by the separation. After all, the situation was forced upon Laura by her husband. She feels she has very few options and numerous restrictions as a result of her husband's actions. Laura's awareness of pending danger relates to unrealistic hopes for reconciliation.

She is then threatened by a vampire and all efforts at defence fail.

Vampire = a warning against excessive negativity and pessimism.
Threat = to feel threatened in a dream is an indication of unexpected setbacks and competition accompanied by devious, underhand behaviour; to threaten someone warns against poor judgement and unfortunate consequences.
Defend = fear of being overwhelmed and overpowered.

The threatening behaviour of the vampire relates to her husband's affair. The deceitful overtones associated with her husband's behaviour have proven unbearable leading to serious insecurities. The fact that Laura does not manage to defend herself successfully suggests that from an emotional point of view, she has to an extent lost control. Next, Laura feels tremendous pain and bleeds excessively.

Pain = emotional disappointment.
Blood = an unfortunate sign, denoting emotional pain and distress.

Both these symbols are associated with emotional disillusionment. Laura is suffering tremendously, currently unable to see a way out of her despair. The use of the pill has a similar connotation.

Pill = depicts a longing to cure and terminate current emotional difficulties.

Laura wonders whether she should take the pill. This refers to a subconscious need to start the healing process through acknowledgement of current disappointments and an examination of plausible solutions. She then finds the pill bitter in taste. This reveals a reluctance to accept the situation. The imagery has been derived from the saying, 'a bitter pill to swallow'.

Part 2

Then I see myself in an office. I keep looking at my watch. I know I should be sorting my accounts, but I'm no good at maths. I keep thinking I have all these debts and someone's going to get me. I hear these whispers. I look at my clothes. They're still covered in blood. Next something feels different. There's no air. I see my husband. He's changed into a monster. I try to get up, but I can't. I'm still paralysed. I keep thinking there's no air. Then I think he's going to kill me. I'm choking. I wake up palpitating and covered in sweat...'

The second part of the dream starts in an office. Laura constantly looks at her watch.

Office = career-related decisions.
Watch = an emphasis on time as regards current activities.

Time seems to be of huge importance in relation to finding suitable employment. This may be partly due to financial pressures as indicated by the reference to accounts.

Account = difficulties in keeping accounts suggest financial pressure; accounts that are balanced and in order refer to financial rewards through careful planning.

Laura is aware that she must do these accounts but finds the task difficult, mentioning her lack of expertise in mathematics.

Mathematics = financial planning.

This particular set of symbols provides an idea of Laura's attitude and experience in relation to financial matters. There is a suggestion that she is not coping well with

related difficulties. In order to sustain balance she needs methodical planning and procedure, but this seems to be an unfamiliar concept for Laura. Her worries about debts in the dream throw some light on the situation.

Debt = a warning against extravagance.

Given her present circumstances, it may be considered surprising that the subconscious feels the need to warn Laura against extravagance. Since her overall financial situation has deteriorated, one would expect prudence rather than unnecessary expenditure. It is of course possible that this behaviour is a product of both her marriage and the divorce. During the years with her husband, life was comfortable and free from financial concerns. This has left Laura with virtually no experience of a situation that may require careful planning. The trauma of the divorce could also have contributed towards a need for over-spending as indulgence in extravagance is often regarded as the symptom of deeper issues. Another interesting possibility is presented by the mention of whispers.

Whisper = rumour; gossip.

Perhaps Laura is partly driven by keeping up appearance. As distraught as she may be, she still wishes to maintain some sense of decorum in relation to the outside world. Her clothes make a further reference to social conditions.

Clothes = generally clothes can refer to either business or social conditions; a lack of clothes suggests fear of social exposure; old, torn or dirty clothes refer to business difficulties; immaculate clothes denote great success through ambition. See individual items of clothing.

At this point, Laura notices that her clothes are still covered in blood. This implies that feelings of distress and despair have seeped into other areas of her life. The divorce has not only affected her love life, but has caused major disturbances in other areas. Next, Laura feels a change and is aware that there is no air.

Air = clean and pure air signifies clarity of thought and mind; lack of air, polluted air or difficulty in breathing suggests a need to 'clear the air' and adapt a fresh approach towards old problems.

Laura's subconscious is urging her to let go of any obsolete beliefs and ideals and assume a fresh approach. Since Laura is aware that something feels different, it may

be assumed that on some level she realises the inevitability of change in relation to her own situation. She then sees her husband change into a monster.

Monster = an obstacle dream, with an emphasis on feelings of panic, dread and trepidation.

The image of Laura's husband turning into a monster may be analysed in different ways. From a symbolic perspective, it highlights her insecurities as regards the future. On a conscious level, Laura watches a man who has played the part of her husband for thirty years become unrecognisable.

At this point in the dream, once again Laura finds that she is paralysed and unable to move, but this time she is also aware of the lack of air. There is a clear warning that unless she makes a concentrated effort to bring about serious changes, the difficulties associated with her current condition will worsen. There is a suggestion that perhaps the root of her inability to progress lies with the emotional dynamics of the situation. This is emphasised by the fact that she thinks the monster wants to kill her and the feeling of being choked as she awakens.

Kill = a very serious warning depicting enemies and much antagonism. Choke = resentment towards an unwanted situation.

Laura's resentment as regards being forced into a divorce has produced so much anger and negativity that it has almost proved impossible to initiate any form of progression or advancement.

Conclusion

This recurring nightmare has been instigated to provoke Laura into regaining control of her life. The difficulties associated with her current condition are abundantly clear and while it is not the intention of the subconscious to detract from her pain, it can no longer sustain or tolerate the continuous emotions of despair and pessimism. Laura's life appears to have come to a standstill with no real direction and very little effort towards instigating change. By accepting the reality of her divorce, Laura can gently initiate the process of healing which would eventually induce a more acceptable conclusion to an unpleasant situation.

Dictionary

Abacus Order through careful financial planning.

Abandon Any form of abandonment indicates a fear of underachievement and a sense of emotional inadequacy.

Abattoir Threat of public exposure and humiliation.

Abbess To meet one suggests peace and tranquillity especially after a period of struggle.

Abbey Signifies devotion. The more interesting and formidable the structure, the greater the emphasis on loyalty and dedication.

Abdicate Upheaval; uncertainty.

Abdomen Refers to 'gut' feeling. A pain in the abdomen is a warning not to ignore one's instincts.

Abduct To be taken by force suggests that courage is required to overcome obstacles.

Aberration A generally fatalistic period ahead; unusual circumstances.

Abhor Having to tolerate undesirable situations; lack of control.

Abide A need to sacrifice for the greater good.

Abode Familiar surroundings refer to progress, especially in business. New territories signify a change in direction.

Abortion Major decisions as regards emotional issues.

Abroad Excitement; new opportunities.

Abrupt Any sudden movement suggests a need for quick and decisive thinking in response to unexpected events.

Abscess An uncomfortable situation that needs to be addressed.

Abscond A warning of lies and treachery.

Absence To be aware of the absence of a loved one suggests clarity in relationships and an understanding of one's emotional needs.

Absentmindedness Carefree times ahead.

Absinthe Buying or drinking absinthe refers to love matters and indicates an interesting, but complicated situation.

Absolution A need for harmony with an emphasis on the importance of truth.

Abstain To refrain from something signifies decisions that are based on logic.

Absurdity A time for light-heartedness; a desire for freedom of expression.

Abundance An overwhelming sense of wealth and affluence is a reminder not to get complacent.

Abuse To dream of being abused indicates a need to take control of a situation. To inflict abuse suggests inner struggle and a fear of defeat.

Abyss   A reluctance to confront obstacles; deep-rooted fears.

Academy   Any form of education or training signifies a time for change and development and an enjoyment of new activities.

Accelerate   Speed usually indicates excitement and emotional gratification.

Accent   News and communication are of great importance.

Accept   Suggests a necessity for reconciliation where there has been conflict and separation.

Accident   Depending on the severity of the accident, this is a warning of unforeseen obstacles.

Acclaim   A need for approval; the emphasis lies with the fear of underachievement.

Accommodate   Success as a result of compromise.

Accompany   This points to the satisfactory conclusion of a difficult situation.

Accomplish   An exceptionally favourable symbol, denoting success and contentment.

Accounts   Difficulties in keeping accounts suggest financial pressure. Accounts that are balanced and in order refer to financial rewards through careful planning.

Accumulate   Signifies a desire for greater diversity.

Accuse   To accuse others suggests frustration; to be accused indicates anxiety and a rather defeatist attitude.

Ache   A warning of emotional conflict; the more severe the sensation, the greater the emphasis on the difficulties ahead.

Acid   Caution is required, particularly in friendships and new partnerships.

Acorn   Success in business matters.

Acquaintance   This implies a rather hesitant approach towards new opportunities. A leap of faith is required.

Acquiescence   An extremely favourable symbol, suggesting balance and harmony in personal relationships.

Acquisition   A need to be more assertive and ambitious.

Acquitted   Forgiveness is required in order to instigate healing.

Acrobat   A more multi tasked approach could prove beneficial.

Acting   A desire to escape the mundane.

Actor   Famous personalities generally represent aspects of one's own dreams and desires. For example, an actor associated with action roles can express the need for a more exciting lifestyle; an actor affiliated with romantic parts could represent one's inner hopes and yearnings for love. Actors associated with evil or villainous roles usually refer to a fear of remaining unfulfilled in relation to certain goals and aspirations.

Adamant   Perseverance is crucial in order to thrive and flourish.

Adapt   Unity and team work will produce great results.

Address   Signifies discussions around the home and family.

Admire   Exciting times ahead, filled with new adventures and emotional gratification.

Adopt A more harmonious state of being is called for with an emphasis on the ability to give and receive.

Adornment A sense of fulfilment and gratitude is indicated.

Adrift This usually refers to serious issues that have not yet been properly addressed. Often the root of these problems stems from childhood insecurities.

Adultery To commit adultery refers to weakness and a tendency to hide from problems; to be aware of someone else committing adultery points to a difficult challenge and strength in adversity.

Adventure A more light-hearted approach to certain situations can prove beneficial.

Adversary This can imply hidden opposition in business.

Adversity Difficulties that need courage and meticulous planning to overcome.

Advertisement Any form of advertising refers to unexpected news and communication.

Advice To give advice suggests a need to listen to one's instincts; to receive advice places the emphasis on the importance of accepting help from others.

Airplane To fly in an airplane indicates outside help may be required in order to set oneself free from a binding situation.

Affection To show, feel or receive affection is a sign of happy social times; to lack affection prompts a reassessment of one's values and priorities.

Affliction Fear of rejection and failure.

Affluence Period of peace and prosperity ahead.

Africa Suggests unexpected circumstances that can provoke great vigour and stimulation.

Afternoon A need for rest and recuperation.

Age Any age related issues have a bearing on the significance of time in relation to certain events.

Agnostic A warning not to lose sight of spiritual needs.

Agony Conflict and dilemma; a situation that needs careful handling.

Agreement Any form of agreement is indicative of a satisfactory resolution after a period of doubt and uncertainty.

Agriculture Extra attention to diet is recommended.

Air Clean and pure air signifies clarity of thought and mind; lack of air, polluted air or difficulty in breathing suggests a need to 'clear the air' and adopt a fresh approach towards old problems.

Alabaster Denotes an appreciation of beauty and an interest in creative activities.

Alarm Any alarm device prompts attention to detail.

Album Issues regarding friends and family.

Alcohol As a drink, it is a warning to avoid excessive behaviour; as a disinfectant it recommends a time for purification.

Algebra Analysis of a troublesome situation can lead to favourable results.

Alibi Remorse; a need to accept past actions.

Alien New meetings through unusual circumstances.

Alimony Contracts involving financial gain.

Alliance A time for more social activity.

Alligator Integration; a flexible utilisation of attributes.

Allowance A sense of joy through sharing and receiving.

Alloy Combining metals refers to happy unions and marriage.

Almond To see almonds points to a period of intense social activity; to eat almonds suggests a longing for more excitement.

Alone To enjoy being alone points to a need for peace and tranquillity; to be left alone by force or to feel lonely indicates emotional upheaval.

Alphabet Exciting career opportunities and new beginnings.

Altar A favourable sign, suggesting trust and hope.

Altitude A broader vision of a difficult situation is called for.

Amazement To be amazed by something portends wonderful surprises ahead.

Ambassador Great social success.

Amber A situation involving a major relationship will be of paramount importance.

Ambition Refers to hidden desires.

Ambulance The focus lies on situations where time is of great importance.

Ambush A warning to be more vigilant; hidden enemies.

America Self employment; interesting ways to make money.

Amethyst A need to listen to advice, especially where love matters are concerned.

Ammonia A danger of unnecessary risks.

Amorous A dream of wish fulfilment, indicating a yearning for love and affection.

Amulet Assistance is required in making a major decision.

Ammunition A warning not to confide too much; discretion is required.

Amputation Suggests a fear of loss and a need to regain control.

Amusement Much fun and happy times ahead.

Anarchy A need to re-evaluate purpose and direction in life.

Ancestors An indication of love and protection.

Anchor Major decisions; much care and deliberation are required.

Angel A wonderful omen denoting focused intentions, achievement of goals and fulfilment of wishes.

Anger In any format, anger depicts difficulties; it all also refers to much inner struggle and a sense of guilt.

Angling A need for rest and recuperation.

Anguish Indicates much doubt as regards an emotional situation.

Animals Any form of fun and enjoyment in relation to animals signifies peace and harmony; to be

attacked by animals is a clear sign of treachery and emotional discord; to hear animals suggests unexpected situations ahead; to feed animals emphasises the need for more compassion and understanding.

Ankle   Refers to hidden cravings.

Anniversary   Family matters are of utmost importance.

Announcement   Depicts communication in relation to business matters.

Annoy   Highly charged situations that need much patience to resolve.

Annulment   A marriage that has been annulled indicates disagreements within a relationship.

Ant   Ants at work suggest industriousness and much success in business. Any problem with ants recommends caution as regards new partnerships.

Antarctic   Time alone is required to reflect on an emotional situation.

Anteater   Refers to obstacles in business.

Antelope   A need to set plans into motion.

Anthem   Diverse and colourful experiences that stimulate the imagination.

Antiques   The necessity to analyse, understand and learn from previous experiences.

Antiseptic   Healing of old wounds; purification.

Anxiety   Doubts about one's own abilities.

Ape   The emphasis lies with family matters and social interaction.

Apology   To apologise suggests a need for self-forgiveness; to be apologised to raises the question of trust in connection to friendships.

Apparition   The importance of looking beneath the surface is highlighted.

Appendicitis   Fear of unexpected problems.

Appetite   A sign of enjoyment and pleasure.

Applause   Suggests success and reward after a period of hard work and determination.

Apple   Sexual desires.

Appointment   A need for order and discipline.

Apprentice   An important time for being receptive and open to new experiences.

Apricot   Contentment and prosperity is denoted.

Apron   Domestic matters need attention; avoid clutter.

Aquamarine   This particular jewel indicates emotional stirrings and the beginning of a relationship.

Aquarium   Emphasises the importance of looking beyond the obvious.

Arbitration   Difficulties can be surmounted with reason and logic.

Arch   Anything in the shape of an arch relates to love matters and advises caution.

Archbishop   More advice and information is required before proceeding with any new venture.

Architect   To become an architect signifies excitement in relation to already existing plans; to encounter one indicates promotion and greater business prospects.

Archives   Reunions; pleasant encounters.

Arctic   A time to reassess personal ambitions.

Arena   Business-related gatherings.

Argue   Any form of argument suggests hostility and opposition.

Arithmetic   Much hard work is required in order to achieve satisfactory results.

Arm   Relates to personal relationships.

Armour   Fears of inadequacy.

Army   Difficulties and disputes ahead.

Arrest   Unfulfilled ambitions; a need for more prowess and determination to achieve goals.

Arrival   Signifies the realisation of long-held dreams.

Arrow   Beware of hasty decisions; real success depends upon patience and perseverance.

Arsenic   A warning of superficial friends and hidden motives.

Arson   Unforeseen problems.

Art   Depicts appreciation and enjoyment.

Arthritis   fear of losing one's independence.

Artichoke   A healthier lifestyle is recommended.

Artist   To be in the company of an artist suggests pleasurable gatherings; to be an artist highlights an emotional awakening.

Asbestos   Hidden enemies.

Ascend   To ascend with difficulty emphasises the necessity for a more assertive attitude; to ascend and reach one's goal indicates success and achievement.

Ashes   Regret as regards an emotional situation.

Asia   A desire to explore and enhance one's sense of spirituality.

Asleep   To be asleep signifies a need to retreat from an emotionally challenging situation; to see others asleep recommends a more detailed examination of family problems.

Asparagus   A closer look at financial matters may be useful.

Asphalt   Travel is depicted.

Aspirin   Represents a period of calm after much hectic speculation.

Assassin   A warning of self-induced difficulties.

Assault   Any form of assault represents a betrayal of secrets.

Asthma   Signifies a suffocating emotional situation that needs to be addressed.

Astrology   Refers to unexpected events that lead to positive changes.

Asylum   A warning not to be distracted by external events and opinions.

Atheist   A need to reassess a problematic situation and explore alternative options.

Athlete   An extremely positive sign, suggesting adventure and excitement.

Atlas   Refers to commercial matters and highlights the significance of

variety and expansion.

Atom   Attention to detail may prove crucial.

Atrocity   A warning not to ignore a pressing situation.

Attic   The focus lies on the importance of recreational activities.

Auction   A reminder not to underestimate talents and capabilities.

Audience   Depicts achievement and approval.

Author   A desire to relive or rewrite certain aspects of the past.

Authority   A fear of circumstances beyond one's control.

Autumn   Positive domestic changes.

Avalanche   Anxiety; turmoil.

Avarice   Loss through indiscreet behaviour.

Avenue   A conscious desire to alter one's dreams and objectives.

Aviary   Useful and interesting social connections.

Awaken   A realisation of potential; promising outlook.

Award   Whether receiving or giving an award, this indicates increased prosperity and personal achievement.

Axe   A warning not to react hastily.

ℬ

Baby   Points to the implementation of new plans and projects.

Back   Greater precautionary measures are recommended in conjunction with career moves.

Backbone   Represents bravery and courage.

Bacteria   A warning not to allow trivial annoyances to escalate and develop into grossly exaggerated problems.

Bad   Any form of behaviour or event that feels bad, signifies treachery in unexpected places.

Badge   Points to an inner search for identity and individuality.

Badger   Success is very much dependant upon greater determination and tenacity.

Bag   An indication of hidden possibilities and subtle overtures.

Bail   Denotes an unexpected resolution to an incredibly difficult situation.

Bailiff   Signifies stressful interference and intrusion.

Bake   Any form of baking refers to pleasurable interludes and intimate gatherings.

Bakery   To be aware of a bakery points to comfortable social interaction.

Balance   Any problems as regards maintaining balance represent discord and confusion, particularly in financial matters; should balance be restored and maintained, clear thinking and logical solutions should be applied to resolve any problematic issues.

Ball   To go to a ball is a sign of new romantic encounters; to play with a ball or be involved in any sport that includes a ball indicates much needed new challenges and opportunities.

Balloon   An enjoyment of pastimes and hobbies.

Ballot   It is important to pay closer attention to all available options with a view to change and reform.

Balm   This suggests physical sensitivity and minor ailments that may well have been induced by stressful conditions.

Bamboo   Implementation of thoughts and ideas.

Banana   Points to a new emotional development with unusual scope and possibility.

Bandage   A sign of continuous disruptions leading to vulnerability.

Banish   Time to face long-held insecurities despite uncomfortable overtures.

Bank   A need for better structure and organisation as far as business and financial matters are concerned.

Bankruptcy   Denotes a fear of shame and exposure.

Banner   An obsessive desire to be acknowledged and accepted.

Banquet Signifies an important formal gathering.

Baptism A sense of gentle healing and spirituality.

Bar Social environments tend to depict light relief and leisure activities.

Barber Represents traditional interests.

Bargain Emphasises the importance of weighing up all relevant options.

Barge A sign of carefree pleasures and emotional contentment.

Barn An appreciation of simplicity; an unpretentious approach.

Barrage An indication of animosity and uncomfortable relationships, particularly within the work environment.

Barren Anything appearing or feeling excessively barren in a dream is a sign of unfulfilled desires and sexual frustration.

Barricade A need to be extremely alert and cautious against hidden opponents.

Barter Recommends greater shrewdness and a more discerning approach in business matters.

Basement This particular area primarily concentrates on hidden fears and inhibitions.

Bath Highlights the importance of emotional purification.

Bathroom Depending on the context, the bathroom can deal with a variety of issues; however, in all cases the emphasis lies with the need to cleanse and dispose of a particular situation to proceed to the next level.

Battle An indication of business-related disagreements.

Battlefield Refers to an important meeting, aimed at resolving disputes.

Bazaar A positive sign, pointing to a period of intrigue and adventure.

Beach A desire for greater diversion and recreation.

Beacon A warning against misunderstandings.

Bead Closer attention to detail can prove useful, particularly in love matters.

Bear Promotes a period of reflection and introspection.

Beard Individuality; choice.

Beauty To be aware of beauty in a dream may be construed as extremely positive as it indicates great joy and fulfilment.

Beaver A sign of productivity and construction.

Bed An important decision.

Bedroom The emphasis lies on love and relationship issues.

Bee Hope and optimism.

Beg An indication of major challenges, particularly within relationships.

Beggar Denotes a period of emotional hardship and desolation.

Belt Represents financial issues and recommends greater attention to expenditure.

Bereavement A reluctant acceptance of separation or divorce.

Bet Depicts a misguided interest in ventures and enterprises that may be riddled with hidden risk and uncertainty.

Bible   Spiritual awakening.

Bicycle   A more concentrated observation of basic plans and designs can prove beneficial.

Bilingual   A need to be more open and understanding towards different views and opinions.

Bin   Emotional baggage that has so far remained unresolved.

Bird   Generally in dreams birds represent hopes and aspirations.

Birth   The beginning of an exceptionally creative and inventive period.

Birthday   An emphasis on significant times and events, particularly in relation to childhood influences.

Biscuit   Points to a recognition of childhood hopes and aspirations.

Bite   Unforeseen treachery.

Bitter   An indication of lies and disappointment.

Bittersweet   Reluctant compromise and a hollow victory.

Black   The colour black represents the unknown and mysterious quantities within any given situation.

Blackmail   A strong warning against deceit and rivalry.

Bladder   Instinctive reaction.

Blame   Overwhelming feelings of guilt and regret.

Bland   Boredom; monotony.

Blanket   Signifies warmth and wellbeing.

Blemish   Fear of ruin and disgrace; sullied reputation.

Blessing   A wonderful omen, denoting peace and happiness.

Blind   An indication of difficulties and an emphasis on the necessity of clear, unbiased judgement as regards a delicate situation.

Blood   An unfortunate sign, denoting emotional pain and distress.

Blue   Signifies spiritual awakening and healing.

Bluff   A more astute and cunning approach is recommended.

Blush   Relates to an awareness of pleasurable sensations and immense physical attraction within a relationship.

Boast   A warning not to reveal too many designs and ideas until greater research has taken place.

Boat   The fragile beginnings of a romance.

Boil   To boil something in a dream suggests much time and analysis is required before a decision can be reached.

Bomb   An unexpected event that can cause uneasiness and commotion.

Bone   An indication of the essential components within a situation.

Book   Acquiring knowledge through wisdom and experience.

Boots   Important financial investments.

Boredom   Implies much discontent and frustration.

Bouquet   An intricate analysis of emotional data within an existing relationship.

Boy   The male aspect in a particular situation.

Box   Represents an episode or a crucial event that the subconscious needs to focus on.

Bracelet   Points to sincerity and genuine intentions within a relationship.

Brain   Depicts intellectual interest and involvement.

Brake   Caution against hasty decisions.

Brass   Modesty and humility.

Bravery   To show bravery is a sign of victory through belief and honesty; to see bravery in others is an indication of emotional support.

Bread   Nourishment; sustenance.

Break   To break something in a dream denotes a parting of ways.

Breast   Maternal issues.

Breathe   Living life to its fullest.

Bribe   To bribe someone warns against self-doubt and insecurity in business affairs; to be bribed is an indication of unsafe plans due to external interference and incompetence.

Bride   An enjoyment of solid, traditional values and beliefs.

Bridge   Mutual consideration and compromise.

Bronze   A desire for higher aims and objectives.

Brooch   Sentimental feelings; past relationships.

Broom   A need to reassess current or pending domestic changes.

Brothel   On an emotional level, this could refer to secret liaisons, such as extra-marital affairs; however, depending on the other details seen in the dream a brothel could also be used to signify questionable financial transactions.

Brother   Representative of close male ties and relations.

Brown   Promotes a down-to-earth and practical approach.

Bruise   Overwhelming feelings of pain and torment.

Bucket   A closer inspection of domestic plans is necessary.

Buffalo   Represents gratitude and answered prayers.

Building   Relates to goals and objectives.

Bullet   Aggressive thoughts and tendencies.

Burn   Clearing of the past; yearning for a fresh slate.

Bury   A need to move on and accept change.

Bus   Teamwork; unity.

Butcher   Signifies emotional issues that require dissection and analysis.

Butter   Smooth exchange and interaction.

Butterfly   Transformation.

Button   Crucial detail.

Buy   To buy something in a dream highlights an interest in expansion and development.

C

Cactus   Irritation; minor difficulties.

Cabbage   An enjoyment of the simpler aspects of life.

Cabin   A new opportunity that may lead to an extensive range of options.

Cabinet   A time to reassess and re-evaluate long-held principles.

Café   An unexpected reunion.

Cage   Trauma; guilt.

Cake   Celebration; emotional contentment.

Calendar   Significant events ahead.

Calico   A warning not to place material welfare above integrity and honesty.

Call   To hear your name being called, suggests your opinions and advice are greatly respected by others; to call someone stresses the need for more sensitivity and understanding.

Calm   An indication of serenity and happiness.

Camel   Refers to the necessity for endurance and stamina.

Camera   Deception; illusion.

Camomile   A desire for peace and tranquillity.

Camp   Teamwork and better management will yield the desired effect.

Campaign   A period of continuous activity and commitment.

Canal   An emotional journey.

Canary   Happy news.

Cancer   To dream of having cancer refers to unresolved problems that are directly and constantly affecting everyday life; to see another person with cancer suggests worry and guilt caused by the inability to face one's fears.

Candle   A search for the truth.

Candy   Denotes an emotionally fulfilling love life.

Cane   Fear of humiliation.

Cannibalism   Warns of illness.

Cannon   Refers to unexpected challenges, rivalry and opposition.

Canoe   Much courage is required to confront an emotionally charged period.

Canopy   Environmental changes.

Cap   Traditional values.

Capsule   Further guidance and assistance would be useful as regards a business situation.

Captain   Decisions that demand careful handling.

Captive   A situation that can cause shame and embarrassment.

Car   Career matters are highlighted.

Cardigan   A need to become more assertive and protect against vulnerability.

Cards   Indicates fatalistic events.

Caress   Recuperation from emotional trauma.

Cargo   Refers to travel, especially for business purposes.

Carnival   A new love affair, filled with passion and excitement.

Carol   Denotes clarity and spiritual harmony.

Carpenter   Nurturing of talents and creativity.

Carpet   Highlights a financial situation.

Carriage   The focus lies within an already existing relationship.

Carrot   Caution against deception and temptation.

Carry   To be aware of carrying something stresses the need to unburden; to see others carrying, indicates difficulties in facing the truth.

Carve   A desire to establish and prove one's capabilities.

Cash   Suggests that basic financial needs will be met.

Casserole   A family dispute that will take time to resolve.

Castle   Long-held dreams and ambitions that will become reality.

Cat   A more confidant and detached approach towards a partnership can instigate beneficial results.

Caterpillar   Life-changing events.

Cathedral   An extremely favourable omen suggesting great success and reward as a result of selfless deeds.

Cattle   Denotes prosperity and prestige.

Cauliflower   Domestic happiness is indicated.

Cave   It is important to pay attention to all repetitive thoughts and feelings provoked by a sense of intuition.

Ceiling   Refers to the more dominant aspects of the personality.

Celebration   Renewal; hope.

Celery   A more vigorous lifestyle could prove beneficial.

Cellar   Inhibition; hidden desires.

Cement   Examination of hard facts.

Cemetery   Recent obstacles and apprehensions will be resolved.

Certificate   Achievement of goals.

Cesspool   A need to dissociate from unwanted thoughts and negative behaviour.

Chain   A craving to break free from the mundane.

Chair   The focus lies on much desired time alone to reflect and meditate.

Chairman   Represents responsibility and obligation.

Chambermaid   More attention to detail is required.

Chameleon   Illusion; camouflage.

Champagne   An eminent sense of triumph.

Champion   An assertive frame of mind.

Chandelier   Clarity; Realisation.

Change   Exploration of options.

Chapel   Renewed hope; faith in the future.

Charade   Fear of social inadequacy and awkwardness.

Charcoal   Passion; fulfilment of dreams.

Chariot   Courage; victory through determination.

Charity   Achievement through compassion and sensitivity.

Chart   Emphasises the importance of goals and objectives.

Chase   Obstacles and setbacks that require attention and planning to resolve.

Chastise Fear of rejection.
Chatter A yearning to unload and unburden.
Cheek Refers to emotional issues.
Cheat Secrets that can cause embarrassment.
Cheer A wonderful sign denoting accomplishment and attainment.
Cheetah Swift advancement.
Cheese Domestic changes.
Chemist Consulting an expert may prove useful.
Cheque To write a cheque suggests a need to examine certain financial matters; to receive a cheque denotes decisive and positive financial news.
Cherry Sexual enjoyment.
Chess The start of provocative new challenges.
Chew It is important to deliberate and think carefully before making any decisions.
Chicken Domestic matters need to be addressed.
Chicken pox Resurfacing of childhood anxieties.
Chilblain Minor irritations.
Child Children represent thought and ideas that need nurturing.
Childbirth Major changes and transformations.
Chimney A need to clear the mind.
Chiropodist It is crucial to act without further delay.
Chisel Tenacity may prove to be the key to success.
Chocolate The focus is on love-related issues.
Choir Spiritual harmony.

Choke Resentment towards an unwanted situation.
Christ A wonderful dream, suggesting love and protection.
Christening Healing old wounds.
Christmas Family gatherings.
Christmas tree A brightly lit and decorated Christmas tree refers to unexpected family reunions. Should the tree appear mundane or damaged, there is a longing for closer family bonds.
Church Spiritual awakening.
Cider Rest and relaxation is recommended; more contact with nature would prove helpful.
Cigar Assertion; making a statement.
Cigarette Old habits and patterns need to be addressed.
Circle Intuition; female issues.
Circus Unusual events.
City A desire to expand and experiment.
Clairvoyant Unexpected circumstances that require much thought and deliberation.
Class Utilising newly acquired information.
Clean An extremely positive omen, suggesting healing, recovery and a renewed sense of purpose.
Clergy Denotes excellent advice from loved ones.
Cliff Uncertainty; insecurity.
Climb Trials and tribulations.
Clock Projects and activities that require time to develop.
Clogs A desire to enjoy the more fundamental aspects of life.

Clothes   Generally clothes can refer to either business or social conditions; a lack of clothes suggests fear of social exposure; old, torn or dirty clothes refer to business difficulties; immaculate clothes denote great success through ambition. *See also individual items of clothing.*

Cloud   Hopes and wishes.

Clown   The focus remains on the necessity to adapt a more light-hearted attitude.

Coal   A sense of gratitude and contentment.

Coat of arms   Family expectations.

Coax   A longing to let go of inhibitions.

Cobbler   A warning against extravagance and waste.

Cobweb   A time for creativity and a more industrious attitude.

Cocoa   Enjoyment of life's comforts.

Coconut   A relationship that is not completely in the open.

Coffee   A time for action and movement.

Coffin   Fear of stagnation.

Coin   Gradual career advancement.

Cold   Apprehension; restlessness.

Collar   Fear of letting go.

Collect   Reassessment; revaluation.

College   Exciting new opportunities leading to expansion.

Colours   Represent moods and emotions; *see also individual colours.*

Collision   Fear of losing control; impetuous, impulsive behaviour.

Combat   Unforeseen difficulties.

Comb   A craving for greater emotional excitement and stimulation.

Comet   Circumstances beyond one's control.

Comfort   A longing to escape from problems.

Command   Danger of feeling overwhelmed.

Compass   A major need to review one's direction.

Complexion   A clear complexion denotes health and happiness; complexion that appears ill or disfigured relates to emotional instability and problematic health issues.

Compliment   To receive a compliment points to accomplishment; to give compliments promotes the necessity for greater focus and clarity.

Computer   Normally, computers symbolise the accumulation and utilisation of knowledge. To have difficulty in using a computer suggests a need for greater perception and receptivity.

Confession   Revelation of secrets.

Confetti   Much delight and gratification.

Confront   Opposition and defiance.

Confuse   Major decisions that may prove perplexing.

Congratulate   A sign of festivities ahead.

Conscience   A clear conscience indicates a sense of relief and an enhancement of the senses. A troubled conscience suggests that much more reflection and self-analysis are required.

Consent   Seeking approval; an urge to impress.

Content Inner peace and serenity.
Contradiction Resentment; envy.
Convict An extremely problematic situation that requires great care and courage to resolve.
Cook The focus lies upon family relationships.
Copper A warning to avoid excess and greed.
Copy Repetition of past events.
Coral Cycles of nature.
Cork Boundaries; limitations.
Corn Enjoyment of the moment.
Corpse Loss of confidence and morale; fear of underachievement.
Cosmetics Improvement; outside assistance.
Cotton Purity; innocence.
Cough A longing for release from unwanted conditions.
Country A representation of dreams and ambitions that are within reach and can be fulfilled.
Countryside Refers to emotional matters.
Court Business disputes.
Courtship A new understanding; progress.
Cow Making the most of what is available.
Cradle Safety and security.
Crawl An exciting development in an already existing relationship.

Cream Opulence; wealth.
Crime Enemies; hidden danger.
Crochet Traditional values.
Cross Protection.
Crossroads A difficult choice.
Crow Destiny.
Crown Empowerment; victory.
Crucify Sacrifice for the greater good.
Cruelty A need to examine values and principles.
Crutches Obstacles; feeling restrained.
Cry Frustration; helplessness.
Crystal A more concise approach is required.
Cucumber Vitality; overall wellbeing.
Cup A measure of emotional contentment; a full cup denotes prosperity; an empty cup points to cold and sterile conditions.
Cupboard Order and organisation can help eliminate current difficulties.
Curse Bitterness; anger.
Curtain A situation that needs to be unveiled.
Cushion Gentle pampering is recommended.
Custard Friendship; strong emotional ties.

Daffodil   A new beginning; fresh outlook.

Dagger   Enemies; betrayal.

Dance   Realisation of long-held dreams and ambitions.

Danger   Signifies unrealistic expectations.

Darkness   Fear of the unknown.

Dawn   Denotes exciting new ventures.

Deafness   A lack of understanding; upheaval.

Death   To fear death suggests anxiety in a relationship; to have a calm attitude towards death indicates a natural conclusion to an emotional situation.

Debt   A warning against extravagance.

Decapitate   Loss of control.

Decorate   Depicts drastic changes.

Deer   A situation that requires sensitivity and gentleness to resolve.

Defend   Fear of being overwhelmed and overpowered.

Deformed   Indicates emotional damage.

Delicate   A warning to avoid harsh situations.

Delight   Sensual pleasures.

Delirium   Points to unwanted external influences.

Dentist   Recommends an examination of health issues.

Descend   A swift resolution concerning business matters.

Desert   Isolation; fear of abandonment.

Desk   The application of wisdom and experience for the purpose of achieving advancement.

Dessert   An indication of future happiness and prosperity.

Destroy   A warning not to act in haste; a necessity for control and restraint.

Detective   An intriguing situation.

Detest   Disruptions and limitations within a relationship.

Devil   A severe warning of strife and conflict.

Diamond   An extremely important love affair.

Dice   Unexpected financial events.

Dictionary   Alternative avenues should be explored.

Die   A prominent sign of change; a desperate urge for emotional detachment in a highly charged situation.

Difficulty   Refers to fears of underachievement.

Dig   A desire to find an appropriate solution.

Diploma   An exciting career opportunity.

Dirt   Generally, soil depicts new possibilities for advancement; should anything appear dirty however, there is a suggestion of unwanted rumours and scandal.

Disability Restrictions; constraint.
Disaster Caution is recommended before undertaking new projects.
Disappointment Regret over past actions.
Disease Emotional discord; a lack of mental stability.
Disgrace Fear of exposure; secrets.
Disguise A situation that demands discretion.
Dishonest Any form of dishonesty refers to dilemma and uncharacteristic disruptions.
Disinfectant Purification of the mind and body is recommended.
Disobedience A wish to escape from the mundane.
Dispute Refers to legal situations that may need careful handling.
Distance To be aware of distance suggests a need for greater patience
Distress Indicates inner conflict and a longing to break free.
Distrust A warning to pay closer attention to instinct and intuition.
Dive It is important to be more forceful and dynamic and less hesitant.
Divorce Detachment from ineffective conditions; embracing new ideas.
Doctor More information is required in order to solve an existing problem.
Dog Loyalty; trust.
Dolphin Playful endeavours; spiritual contentment.
Donkey Perseverance; success through hard labour.
Door Important new opportunities that can induce significant changes.
Dove Purity; innocence.

Dragon Deep-rooted beliefs; tradition.
Draw A strong indication of emotional healing.
Dream Analysing different aspects of a puzzling situation.
Dress Emotional issues with an emphasis on female matters.
Drink A desire to include more leisure activates.
Drive Represents progression through life.
Drop Signifies anxiety in relation to fulfilling expectations.
Drown A state of constant dread and turmoil.
Drowsiness A warning to distinguish between reality and illusion.
Drum Communication; news.
Duck More contact with nature and a more natural lifestyle is recommended.
Duet Loyal friends.
Dumb Points to a fear of expression and communication.
Dungeon Emotional entrapment; loss of identity.
Dusk Conclusion; completion of projects.
Dust Disorder.
Dwarf A need to take into account different points of view.
Dye Denotes an incorporation of different ideas.
Dynamite A potentially dangerous situation.

E

Eagle A wonderful omen, suggesting triumph, courage and inspiration.

Ear A need to be more sensitive towards emotional situations; to have earache warns of interference and unnecessary arguments.

Earring Cultural issues.

Earth Accomplishment through a more logical approach.

Earthquake Unforeseen domestic problems.

East Variety; diversity.

Easter A yearning to replenish on all levels.

Eat Any form of eating relates to desire and sexual energy.

Echo A warning not to ignore messages conveyed through instinct or the subconscious.

Eden Examining fundamental ideas.

Eel A love-related situation that may not be all it seems.

Egg Inspiration; new beginnings.

Elastic A need to be more flexible.

Election Different point of view.

Electricity Optimism; light at the end of the tunnel.

Elephant Nurturing instincts.

Elf Childhood memories and experiences.

Elk Stamina; endurance.

Elopement Points to a situation riddled with risk.

Email Swift communication.

Embark An enthusiastic approach towards newly constructed plans.

Embarrassment Represents a guilty conscience.

Embrace A desire to show emotion.

Embroidery A need to focus more on family matters.

Emerald Financial issues surrounding a relationship.

Emigrate Major changes affecting all areas of life.

Emperor Regaining control; confidence in one's abilities.

Employ Employment-related dreams suggest a radical examination of purpose and direction.

Empty To empty out something highlights the importance of letting go when necessary; to see emptiness refers to unfulfilled ambitions.

Enchantment A period of delightful surprises.

Enemy Arguments and hostility.

Engagement A desire for approval and advancement.

Engine A gain in momentum within existing business activities.

Engrave A yearning to demonstrate one's abilities.

Enjoyment A period of spiritual contentment.

Entertainment Celebration; light-hearted pursuits.

Entombment A warning of over-commitment.

Envelope Represents discussions

with a consultant or mediator.

Envy   Harmful friendships.

Eruption   Creativity; renewed vitality.

Escape   Success after much effort and labour.

Eve   Female aspects of a relationship.

Evening   Eventual achievement after much caution and deliberation.

Evidence   Indicates careless, rather haphazard behaviour that leads to problems.

Evil   A serious warning against any involvement in unsavoury activities.

Examination   Essential character-building challenges lie ahead.

Exchange   Denotes the arrival of an unexpected opportunity to accumulate knowledge.

Excitement   A provocative period of much stimulation and gratification in love matters.

Excrement   The significance rests with financial interests and urges a more detailed analysis of any concerns.

Excursion   Escapism; an evasive approach towards undesirable conditions.

Exhausted   A warning not to take on too much responsibility.

Exhibition   Shyness; lack of confidence.

Exile   Fear of deprivation.

Expedition   Great scope for expansion; self-employment.

Explosion   Emotional discord.

Extravagant   Domestic success through good management.

Eye   Spiritual matters; morality.

Eyebrow   Understatement; passive control.

ℑ

Fabric   Foundation; blueprint.

Face   Represents outward appearances.

Factory   Usually dreams involving a factory relate to issues concerning the home front.

Failure   Laziness; lack of inspiration.

Fairy   An extremely positive omen depicting simple pleasures and innocence.

Faith   To have faith in something may be considered as reassurance that help is at hand; to lose faith warns of loss through misjudgement.

Faithful   Any dream concentrating on faithfulness points to a relationship that needs time to heal and repair.

Fake   Suggests problems through dangerous associations.

Fall   This is very much an obstacle dream, relating to specific anxieties.

Fame   A warning of misguided decisions based on negative ego.

Family   An indication of emotional contentment within a given situation.

Famine   Difficult and unexpected financial conditions that need careful handling.

Fanatic   Any excessive enthusiasm denotes impetuous behaviour and questionable decisions.

Farm   Success is dependant upon greater dedication and discipline.

Fashion   Desired results through much innovation and modification.

Fast   Points to renewed excitement and passion.

Fat   Danger of loss through neglect.

Fate   Unusual and mysterious circumstances.

Father   Represents authority.

Fatigue   Warns of an unhealthy lifestyle that can have adverse effects.

Fear   Any fear-related dreams usually point to unresolved emotional issues.

Feast   Satisfactory completion of ongoing projects.

Feather   Confession; release of guilt.

Feline   Generally most animals from the cat family highlight important situations with a bearing on social interaction.

Fence   Represents self-induced obstacles.

Fencing   Promotes tolerance and a less argumentative attitude.

Fertility   An eagerness to take on new challenges.

Fever   Points to heated disputes and a loss of temper.

Fiancé(e)   Highlights the need for stability and greater emotional wellbeing.

Field   Should the field appear planted, it prompts an assessment of recent events. A ploughed field depicts a favourable outcome in relation to current projects. A dry, barren field signifies disappointment through mismanagement.

Fight Much strife and antagonism may be expected.

Film Life review; evaluation of important events.

Find Realisation; a new understanding.

Finger The emphasis lies on versatility.

Finish To finish something successfully denotes prosperity through perseverance. To have difficulty in finishing a task points to opposition and deceitful individuals.

Fire Any situation involving fire refers to love affairs.

Firework Unexpected news; conclusive information.

Fish Dreams involving fish generally relate to feelings and moods.

Fishing A need to maintain greater control in a potentially volatile relationship.

Fix To be fixing anything concentrates on the need to resolve certain problematic details within a specific situation.

Flag Represents pride and achievement.

Flame To be particularly aware of a flame denotes an extremely passionate love affair.

Flash Refers to the discovery of an ideal solution.

Flattery More honesty and sincerity is recommended.

Flatulence Predicament; quandary.

Flea Persistent obstacles.

Flirt A yearning for more fun and carefree pleasure.

Float Points to great strength of character.

Flood A desperate need to unburden.

Floor The focus lies on the actual foundation of any given situation.

Flour A return to basics.

Flower If the flower appears beautiful it portends great love and immense spiritual harmony; should the flower be withered and decaying, it suggests much sadness and regret over past actions.

Fly Represents a desire to escape from the mundane.

Fog A sense of dread and panic in having to face the truth.

Fold A more organised and coordinated approach will yield favourable results.

Folly The importance of adopting a more serious attitude is emphasised.

Food Refers to comfort and pleasure.

Fool Fear of shame and embarrassment.

Foot Recommends a more confident and self reliant state.

Football Deeper involvement in recreational activities can prove beneficial.

Footprint A desire to leave an impression.

Footstep A period of great anticipation.

Forehead A more tolerant and serene frame of mind should be considered.

Foreign Stimulation; provocation.

Forest The unknown.

Forget Feeling inundated by excess responsibility.

Fork A need to dwell and reflect upon all available options.

Forlorn Boredom; lack of inspiration.

Forsake An emotional decision with serious consequences.

Fortress Signifies an unreasonable fear of commitment.

Fossil Suggests an examination of previous relationships.

Fountain A sign of good health.

Fox A time for diplomacy and discretion.

Fragrance Points to an intense alertness of the senses.

Frantic Emotional chaos.

Fraud A warning not to waste time; an unworthy cause.

Freedom An extremely positive omen, denoting fulfilment of wishes.

Freeze A danger of making rash decisions.

Friend A sense of safety and security.

Frog A time for tranquillity and cleansing.

Frost Refers to thoughts and ideas that are reliant on the passage of time to come into fruition.

Frown Depicts minor setbacks.

Fruit Generally most fruit relate to emotional, sexual and love matters. *See also individual fruit.*

Fry Avoid feelings of bitterness and vengeance.

Fuchsia Points to a strong desire to travel.

Fudge Pleasure and gratification.

Fugitive An imminent danger of depression.

Fun Recreational activities.

Funeral Coming to terms with painful issues.

Fungus A need to steer clear of gossip.

Fur A sense of being sheltered from harm.

Furniture If in good condition, furniture suggests domestic serenity; should the furniture appear old, worn or broken, there is a strong urge to resolve neglected domestic concerns.

Future Highlights the need to plan effectively.

G

Gag Intimidation.

Gallery Memories; fragments of past experiences.

Gallop Satisfactory results.

Gambling Secrets; a situation fraught with risk.

Games To indulge in playing games suggests a longing for incentive and arousal.

Gang Searching for identity.

Garden A relationship that needs nurturing.

Garment Development of certain character traits.

Garnet Refers to a love affair that may appear serious but may prove to be not quite as it seems.

Garter Sexual fantasy.

Gather Productivity; an extremely busy and rewarding period ahead.

Germ Deceptive appearances; false friends.

Ghost Recommends further probing of any unusual or puzzling situations.

Giant Blowing things out of proportion; irrational behaviour.

Giddy A longing for a more fulfilling love life.

Gift To give a gift, warns of unnecessary sacrifice within a problematic relationship; to receive a gift points to unexpected ordeals.

Girl Female aspect of any situation.

Glacier An enormous task.

Glass Emphasises focus and vision.

Glasses A need to take into consideration alternative perspectives in order to achieve a clear understanding.

Globe The bigger picture.

Gloom Isolation; unwanted detachment.

Gloves Hidden plans.

Glow Natural attributes.

Glue An awkward situation.

Goat Leadership qualities.

God Perusing perfection; higher purpose.

Gold Mutual understanding; profitable agreement.

Gong The arrival of a fatalistic moment in time.

Goose pimples An exciting episode.

Gospel Religious values; an awakening.

Gossip A warning of self-induced problems.

Gown Represents important social events.

Grain Points to a profitable venture.

Grape Health matters.

Gratitude Successful undertakings.

Grave Fearing a lack of time in relation to the accumulation of wealth.

Green Refers to money matters, in particular financial transactions.

Grey Employment issues.

Groan A recommendation to accept assistance.

Groom Official and legal matters that can prove advantageous.

Ground   Humility; modesty.

Guard   A warning to think carefully before expressing any opinions.

Guest   Denotes an amusing revelation.

Guide   Enjoyable interludes with loyal friends.

Gum   A 'sticky' situation.

Gun   An unfavourable sign, indicating a sense of dread and trepidation.

Gutter   A yearning to improve on existing conditions of living.

Gymnastics   Represents a search for balance and stability.

ℋ

Hail   Annoyance; quarrels.

Hair   Should the hair appear attractive and in good condition, it is a sign of great prosperity and contentment. If the hair appears longer than normal, it signifies gradual advancement and distinction. Hair that is either shorter than usual or brittle suggests a fear of loss and affliction. Dyed hair points to minor changes. Any form of hair loss denotes sad and melancholy circumstances.

Halloween   An amusing opportunity.

Hammer   A busy and constructive period.

Hammock   Tranquillity.

Hand   Attractive hands denote much acclaim and success in career matters.

Hands that have been injured or disfigured point to sacrifice and anguish.

Handbag   Discretion; privacy.

Handcuffs   Refers to unresolved emotional issues.

Handkerchief   Minor health matters.

Handwriting   Greater attention to detail is required.

Hanging   To witness a hanging suggests outside pressure and interference; to be hanging oneself is a warning against over commitment.

Hangover   Excess; out of control behaviour.

Happiness   An exceedingly positive omen, depicting triumph and pleasure.

Harbour   Refers to artistic and creative elements.

Harem   News; gossip.

Harness   Fear of false friendships and entrapment.

Harvest   A successful outcome to an ongoing venture.

Hassock   Seeking greater comfort and wellbeing.

Hat   Points to an event that requires much procedure and protocol.

Hatch   The onset of an interesting cycle.

Hate   Any feelings of hatred refer to disruptive and undesirable relationships.

Hawk   Important news and information.

Hay   A casual encounter.

Head   Dreams relating to the head focus on career matters and quite often predict change.

Headache   Disruptions; unwanted delays associated with business.

Hearse   The end of a situation.

Heart   Relates to relationship issues.

Heat   Excitement; risk.

Heathen   Questioning certain demands and principals within an emotional situation.

Heaven   A happy and fulfilling outcome.

Hedge   Personal boundaries; self-preservation.

Heirloom   Inherited traits and characteristics.

Hell An unfortunate omen, depicting a sense of anguish and desolation.

Helmet A more cautious and vigilant attitude in business is recommended.

Help To ask for help points to an awakening and a true understanding of what is required in order to accomplish and progress; to offer help suggests a need for greater emotional involvement.

Hemp Depicts a period of wellbeing.

Hermit Self-reflection; contemplation.

Hiccough Minor annoyances.

Hide Fear of exposure; weakness and vulnerability.

Hill Setbacks.

Hive Dangerous undertakings.

Hoard A warning not to clutter the mind with unnecessary and potentially harmful thoughts.

Hobby Exploration of new options.

Hoe A time to commit to serious hard work.

Hole Represents inhibitions, phobias and fears.

Holiday A sense of release from worry.

Honey Great contentment in love is depicted.

Honeymoon An important journey.

Honour Reassessment of principals and values.

Hood Hidden agenda.

Hook Refers to feelings of attachment within a relationship.

Hoop An unusual challenge.

Horizon Desire; ambition.

Horoscope An intriguing encounter.

Horse Power; strength.

Hospital A need to recuperate from a painful and traumatic ordeal.

Hotel Interlude; time away from everyday life.

House More often than not, the house depicts a person, with the various rooms representing aspects of the personality as well as life in general. For example, the kitchen relates to domestic matters, while the bedroom focuses on love and relationships. The basement can touch on secrets, fears and inhibitions. Different rooms should be looked at individually as well as with all other relevant details. To move house is a sign of transition and modification.

Hug Generosity.

Hunger Frustration; dissatisfaction.

Hunt Signifies hostility and aggression.

Hurdle Disputes and difficulties that need to be overcome.

Hurricane Unexpected problems causing havoc.

Hurt Any form of physical injury depicts disappointment and anguish; feeling emotionally hurt points to betrayal and deception.

Hurry Restlessness.

Husband Represents the male issues within a relationship.

Hymn A sign of serenity through spiritual belief.

Hypnotism A warning not to misjudge certain situations.

Hypocrite To act in a hypocritical fashion suggests that principles have been compromised for too long; to see hypocritical behaviour in others recommends a closer analysis of existing relationships.

Hysterics Distress; pain.

I

Ice Refers to coldness and frigidity within a relationship.

Iceberg A sense of boredom and inaction, especially where love is concerned.

Ice cream Fun and relaxation.

Idle Danger of complacency.

Idol Searching for the truth.

Ignite A love affair that may prove controversial.

Ignore To ignore anything or anyone indicates a fear of facing certain facts; to be ignored warns against selfishness.

Illegal Points to temptation and the need for much willpower.

Illiteracy Unfulfilled potential.

Illness Lethargy; Listlessness.

Illusion An emphasis on the need for greater observation and scrutiny.

Imitate Denotes a search for alternative solutions.

Immature A sign of thoughtlessness, especially in relationships.

Impale A serious warning, depicting betrayal in love.

Impostor Fear of expressing one's true emotions.

Incense Contentment and gratitude.

Incest A situation that could potentially prove humiliating and distressful.

Income Refers to major opportunities that could eventually lead to a change in career.

Incubate Success through patience and diligence.

Indigo An uncontrollable longing for a more exotic lifestyle.

Inherit Depicts an appreciation of family ties and values.

Injury Disillusionment; disappointment in relationships.

Ink Greater communication skills can prove advantageous.

Inn Home comforts.

Innocence Childhood events and experiences that are still of major importance.

Insanity Heightened emotional tension; vulnerability.

Insect Points to minor disturbances and setbacks.

Insult Anger; loss of control.

Intestines It is important to 'digest' all relevant information before reaching a decision.

Intrigue A tantalising new love affair.

Invest Signifies commitment within a relationship.

Investigate Any form of investigation refers to a need for change and reform.

Invitation Reunions; celebrations.

Irritate A sign of domestic problems.

Iron Highlights a sense of stability and accomplishment within career matters.

Island Individuality; creativity.

Itch A recurring problem that needs to be addressed.

Ivory Financial wellbeing.

J

Jacket   Self-preservation.
Jackpot   Signifies an unexpected windfall.
Jade   Financial gain through creativity.
Jail   Emotional entrapment; blackmail.
Jam   Denotes a sweet and innocent relationship.
Jasmine   Marriage; a desire for commitment.
Javelin   Scope for career expansion.
Jaw   Individuality; expression.
Jealousy   Refers to a disruptive situation filled with confusion and misunderstanding.
Jelly   Participation in fun and simple activities can prove beneficial.
Jeopardy   Danger of undesirable meddling and interference.
Jesus   A wonderful omen depicting love and forgiveness.
Jewel   In most cases, jewellery refers to relationships and love affairs. *See also individual items*.

Journey   Refers to specific events and experiences that may be relevant as regards certain situation.
Joy   A period of peace and contentment.
Jug   Represents a highly emotional situation.
Juggle   The emphasis lies on the need to multi-task.
Jump   A desire to overcome restrictions and obstacles.
Junction   Indicates a major turning point.
Jungle   Facing the unknown.
Junk   Emotional baggage.
Jury   Family situations that demand debate and discussion.
Justice   A sense of divine intervention; order through fatalistic events.

K

Kangaroo Signifies overwhelming emotional attachment.

Karma To be aware of karmic factors suggests wisdom through experience.

Keepsake Refers to a highly emotional interlude.

Kerb Recommends an exploration of alternative options.

Kettle Domestic comfort and wellbeing.

Key Clarity; enlightenment.

Khaki An enjoyment of outdoor activities.

Kick An indication of important decisions that should not be taken lightly.

Kidnap To be kidnapped suggests a need for greater control and assertion as regards a specific relationship; to kidnap someone else points to irresponsible behaviour and an overt fear of commitment.

Kill A very serious warning depicting enemies and much antagonism.

Kilt A traditional celebration.

Kimono Denotes a financially beneficial union.

King Power; figure of authority.

Kiss A desire to love; a longing to share and express emotion.

Kitchen Refers to domestic matters, and depending on the other details involved, focuses on aspirations or problems in this area.

Kite Freedom; liberation from anxiety.

Knee Movement; flow of activity.

Kneel The importance of humility is highlighted.

Knife Represents actions and words that if used unwisely can cause great damage.

Knight Signifies a yearning for greater emotional security within a relationship.

Knit Preparation for the future.

Knock To hear knocking refers to messages and communication; to knock recommends taking initiative and encouraging dialogue.

Knot Danger of being engulfed and embroiled into problematic scenarios.

Knowledge Focuses on the utilisation of wisdom.

Koran Points to the incorporation of spiritual beliefs into daily life.

$\mathcal{L}$

Label It is important to look at the bigger picture and not dwell deeply on trivial details.

Laboratory Learning through trial and error; experimentation.

Labour A need to devote time and energy to unresolved situations.

Labyrinth Mystery; puzzle.

Lace Sensuality; feminine issues.

Ladder An examination of hopes and aspirations.

Lagoon A desire for tranquillity and contemplation.

Lake Focuses on love and relationships.

Lamb Innocence; purity.

Lame An unwanted situation that can lead to setbacks.

Lamp A yearning to throw light on recent events.

Land Represents financial matters and the need to take a closer look at contracts and documents.

Lantern Signifies intuition and points to understanding through inner knowledge.

Latch Commitment issues.

Late To be late or have a fear of being late points to insecurity and confusion.

Laugh Completion of plans and projects.

Laundry Concealed information.

Lavender An excellent indication of healing and recovery.

Law An emphasis on principles and morality.

Lawn Should the lawn appear in good condition, it depicts new friendships and encounters; if the lawn appears withered and dry, it refers to social discontent.

Lawyer A need to accept guidance and advice.

Lazy Lost opportunities through neglect and folly.

Leopard Denotes a rather illusive situation filled with intrigue and fascination.

Leaf Highlights emotional assessment and reaction.

Leak A need to convey thoughts and opinions.

Learn Generally, any form of learning refers to a desire for progress and advancement. However, should the process prove difficult in the dream, this may be regarded as a sign of deep-rooted fears and anxieties that should be confronted and resolved.

Lease Points to temporary conditions and a sense of greater planning for the future.

Leave To leave something or someone in a dream signifies the completion of a particular phase; to be left behind points to a lack of courage in relation to facing crucial facts.

Leather To see leather in a dream indicates that a far more flexible and

versatile attitude is required in order to achieve success.

Lecture   Promotes enlightenment and enjoyment through an accumulation of information.

Leech   A sign of exhaustion and fatigue.

Leek   Recommends a closer look at diet.

Leg   Relates to activity and exertion.

Lemon   An unfortunate sign depicting a bitter discovery accompanied by the exposure of hidden designs and motives.

Lend   To see the act of lending in any context points to problems that may be overcome through teamwork and outside assistance.

Leprosy   An indication of much inner turmoil as well as desolation and confusion.

Lesson   Depicts an important turning point with an emphasis on learning and utilising new skills.

Letter   To receive a letter signifies greater dialogue and communication; to write a letter recommends a more sincere and open approach as regards a particular situation.

Library   Memories; archives of the mind.

Lice   Unwanted visitors.

Lie   A resistance towards accepting the truth.

Lift   Whether lifting anything in a dream or seeing something being lifted, there seems to be an urgent need to unburden in relation to rather troubling circumstances.

Light   Knowledge; wisdom.

Lightening   A fatalistic turn of events.

Lilac   Insight into an emotional situation.

Linen   If the linen appears fresh and clean, honesty and openness in love are depicted; soiled linen points to lies, deceit and infidelity.

Lingerie   Sexual fun and fantasy.

Lion   Family support.

Lips   Prowess; aptitude.

Lisp   Fear of communication; avoiding contact.

Liver   A problem that can be resolved with a change in outlook and attitude.

Lock   Recommends a far more vigilant approach as regards an emotional involvement.

Locket   Precious memories.

Log   Refers to the foundation of an interesting business proposal.

Lonely   Fear of loss and abandonment.

Loom   An indication of constructive activities that would ultimately prove extremely beneficial.

Lorry   Signifies a work-related journey.

Loss   Fear of defeat and ruin.

Lottery   An unusual offer.

Love   Any dream concentrating on love attempts to tackle questions that are of importance in conjunction to the various relationship issues that need to be highlighted. This can include any emotional matter, from marriage and friendship to family.

Loyal   To be aware of loyalty

emphasises the need for greater responsibility and commitment.

Luck Unexpected help and support.

Luggage Travel; change.

Lungs Suggests involvement in outdoor activities.

Lust Weakness; a questionable sense of judgement.

Luxury A longing for improvement and advancement.

Lynx Secrets.

ℳ

Magazine   Seeking information.

Magic   Promotes greater belief in one's own abilities; self-motivation and assurance.

Magistrate   Denotes problematic circumstances that requires the intervention of a third party to resolve and conclude favourably.

Magnet   An indication of overwhelming physical attraction.

Magnifying glass   A more in-depth analysis of an ongoing situation is essential.

Magnolia   Passion; fervour.

Malice   A warning against harbouring a grudge.

Man   Represents masculine influences.

Mane   A sign of sexual prowess.

Manicure   More time and effort should be devoted to self care.

Mansion   Points to a general improvement in circumstances.

Manure   Refers to financial investments that require time and patience to flourish.

Map   Suggests a reassessment of direction and purpose.

Marathon   Stamina; endurance.

Marble   A caution against over-indulgence and extravagance.

Market   Denotes an appreciation of basic pleasures and simplicity.

Marmalade   Signifies a new love interest.

Marriage   Points to an examination of emotional needs and requirements.

Mask   Fear of exposure.

Massage   Releasing tension.

Match   A desire to instigate new activities.

Mathematics   Financial planning.

Mattress   Material welfare.

Meat   Prosperity; a sense of overall wellbeing.

Medal   Seeking recognition.

Medicine   Health-related advice; check-up.

Melancholy   A period of sad reflection.

Melon   Summer fun.

Memory   Awareness of memory-related issues emphasises the necessity to learn from experience.

Mermaid   Imagination; creativity.

Message   Communication from the subconscious.

Metal   A test of courage and determination.

Meteor   An indication of unusual circumstances that may need careful handling.

Microscope   Recommends greater analysis of recent problems.

Mildew   An indication of repetitive irritations.

Milestone   Depicts a significant turn of events which would then be followed by major decisions.

Milk   Relates to basic elementary requirements.

Millstone   Life review; a need to

consider alternative options.

Mine Any mine- or mining-related dreams refer to talents and abilities that are yet to be discovered and utilised.

Minister A need for specialised consultation.

Miracle Faith; strong spiritual beliefs.

Mirage An indication of doubt and uncertainty.

Mirror Self-reflection; a search for the truth.

Mist Signifies a period of upheaval which inevitably instigates a search for direction and purpose.

Mistake Fear of failure and incompetence.

Mole Relates to cosmetic health issues.

Monarch A strong indication of social ambition.

Monastery Denotes spiritual reflection and contemplation.

Money All dreams relating to money focus on proficiency and attitude where financial issues are concerned.

Monk A need for self-analysis and contemplation.

Monster An obstacle dream, with an emphasis on feelings of panic, dread and trepidation.

Moon Feminine intuition.

Mop A time to restart or reset a potentially faded situation.

Morning A new beginning; a fresh outlook.

Mosque Spiritual literature.

Moth Points to the pursuit of knowledge.

Mother Nurturing instincts.

Mountain An endeavour or task that requires perseverance before it can be completed.

Mourning A need for emotional release.

Mouse An undesirable influence.

Mouth Signifies communication and the need to express inner wishes and desires.

Mow It would be of great benefit to tackle external influences and interference.

Mud Difficult endeavours.

Muddle Misgivings; uncertainty.

Multiply Financial gain.

Museum Knowledge through an analysis of past experiences.

Music Any piece of music that is pleasant and in tune points to emotional serenity and spiritual awareness; should the music prove harsh and offensive, a closer inspection of values and principals is recommended. Music instruments refer to personal hopes and preferences.

Mutiny An unexpected turn of events which may prove controversial.

Mystery An indication of hidden blessings.

Mystic Assistance from an unusual source.

𝒩

Nag   Any form of nagging warns against selfish behaviour.

Nail   On fingers and toes, nails relate to the finishing touches in any given situation; should they appear clean or neatly polished, this would indicate a positive outcome where every detail has been considered with tremendous care and deliberation. If the nails appear unsightly, the suggestion would be one of persistent difficulties due to neglect. A nail being hammered into a wall refers to changes on the home front.

Naked   To see oneself naked in a dream points to a fear of exposure; it also highlights growing emotional problems due to a distinct lack of confidence; to see others naked implies that certain truths and realities are about to be revealed.

Name   References to names in dreams highlight situations in conjunction to the people in question; to hear one's own name is a reminder to be more vigilant.

Nap   A time to rest and replenish.

Narrow   Should anything appear unusually narrow, there is a suggestion of restraint and limitation.

Nausea   Inability to make certain emotional decisions.

Navy   Exploration; uncharted territory.

Neck   This part of the body is heavily associated with passion and desire; it also represents the concept of beauty.

Necklace   A casual love affair that may turn serious.

Need   To need anything in a dream is an indication of doubts and misgivings in relation to certain decisions.

Needle   A warning not to ignore relevant details.

Neglect   To neglect anyone or anything is a sign of underachievement through mismanagement; to be neglected points to setbacks due to disorganisation and surrounding incompetence.

Neighbour   A harmonious situation with neighbours denotes an improvement in social circumstances; problems suggest social embarrassment.

Nest   Conditions are ready for change and development.

Net   A need to be more proactive.

News   Unexpected communication.

Newspaper   Searching for the truth.

Night   Completion; ending.

Nightmare   Feeling overburdened; depression.

Nod   Seeking praise and approval.

Noise   Idle gossip.

North   Highlights an awareness of spiritual needs.

Nose   Instinctive reaction.

Numb   Signifies protection against harmful behaviour.

Number Numbers seen in a dream may be regarded as actual and should therefore be analysed in conjunction with the interpretation of all other relevant symbols.

Nun Denotes a sense of sacrifice for the greater good.

Nurse A more compassionate disposition will instigate vast rewards.

Nut A sign of flexibility, especially within social settings.

Oak   A need for greater maturity and understanding.

Oasis   To be in an oasis represents a balanced and harmonious frame of mind; to see an oasis in the distance indicates an inner search for peace and serenity.

Oat   A reference to virility.

Oath   Commitment; undertaking.

Obesity   A warning against excess.

Obey   Routine; discipline.

Obituary   Depicts a situation that has outlived its relevance.

Obligation   A stronger sense of focus and dedication would prove beneficial.

Observe   To be aware of intense observation suggests a review of current plans.

Observatory   Insight; vision.

Ocean   The ocean is indicative of love-related issues.

Odour   A pleasant odour suggests pleasure and gratification; an offensive odour points to a potentially damaging situation.

Offend   To be offended is a sign of harsh, inhospitable conditions in relation to social matters; to offend someone else denotes anger and resentment within a relationship.

Offer   To offer something in a dream indicates an emotionally rewarding interlude; to receive an offer depicts positive external influences.

Office   Career-related decisions.

Ointment   A fragile and sensitive state of mind.

Old   To be aware of something looking old or should any form of ageing be particularly poignant in a dream, the emphasis remains with time and the need to reach important targets within a certain period.

Olive   Social activity.

Onion   Resourcefulness and versatility.

Onyx   Mystery; curiosity.

Opal   Points to the importance of honesty and devotion within a relationship.

Opera   An unexpected diversion.

Operation   An indication that major changes are inevitable; life review.

Opium   A time to confront inner demons.

Oppose   To face opposition signifies unforeseen rivalry and competition; to oppose, suggests suspicion and scepticism in relation to a new proposition.

Optician   Success can be obtained through increased perception and a clearer vision.

Orange   Recommends a closer analysis of any ongoing dietary issues.

Orchid   An unusual and rather controversial love affair.

Ostrich   Status; prestige.

Otter   Heightened feminine instincts.

Outrage   Indicates disbelief and indignation due to the discovery of

malicious, under-hand behaviour.

Oven   Depicts a need to pay closer attention to domestic changes.

Overalls   Protection; damage control.

Overboard   Chaos; upheaval.

Overtake   An ambitious project.

Owl   Refers to intuitive knowledge.

Oyster   An awareness of heightened sexual energy.

Pain Emotional disappointment.

Paint To see paint or to be engaged in any form of painting is indicative of creative stirrings.

Palace An improved standard of living accompanied by a sense of serious accomplishment.

Panic Circumstances that require wit, discretion and a relatively calm disposition to handle effectively.

Panther The unknown quantities that can exist within a relationship are highlighted by the appearance of the panther.

Paper Freedom of choice; decisions yet to be made.

Paralysis Feeling trapped and hindered; restrictions.

Parcel An unexpected opportunity.

Park Recommends a wider range of recreational activities.

Party The lighter side of life.

Passion An extremely positive omen, depicting renewed zest and enthusiasm.

Passport Travel; a longing for adventure.

Pastry A comfortable home environment.

Path Depending on the other details seen in the dream, a path is representative of an important decision and its eventual consequences.

Patch Refers to a significant piece of information that may prove vital in unravelling a puzzling situation.

Patchwork Relevant facts and data.

Pattern To be aware of any definite pattern emphasises the importance of sequence and order in relation to upcoming events.

Pavement Promotes an examination of alternatives.

Pay To pay for something suggests a need to forego certain personal interests in recognition of a higher purpose; to be paid recommends a closer scrutiny of current difficulties.

Peacock Pride; accomplishment.

Pearl Romantic bliss; exceptional happiness.

Pebble Minor obstacles which can be readily overcome.

Pen Signifies a more proactive attitude towards communication.

Penance A guilty conscience.

Pencil An outline of ideas and plans.

Pendulum Routine; procedure.

Pension A need to take into consideration the consequences of any given action.

People To be aware of people in general is indicative of an increase in social activities and interests.

Pepper A craving for greater diversion and excitement.

Perfume Sensuality; attraction.

Peril A warning not to delay taking appropriate action as regards certain decisions.

Perspire   Points to an extremely busy and involved period.

Pest   An unexpected disagreement.

Pesticide   Greater assertion may be required to successfully resolve a dispute.

Petal   Fragility; sensitivity.

Petrol   An essential component within a situation.

Pewter   Reflection; diplomacy.

Phantom   A sense of dread and anguish.

Pharmacy   Represents information and expertise.

Photograph   A review of past events and experiences.

Picnic   An appreciation of simplicity.

Picture   Fragments of the past and their effect on current conditions.

Pie   Refers to emotional objectives.

Pig   An indication of controversy and disagreement.

Pigeon   Signifies an interesting reunion.

Pilgrim   Seeking greater spiritual expression and liberation.

Pill   Depicts a longing to cure and terminate current emotional difficulties.

Pillow   A superficial relationship.

Pilot   Represents a figure of trust.

Pin   A warning against pending danger.

Pineapple   A period of rest and recuperation.

Pink   An emphasis on love and relationships.

Pirate   Refers to a secret liaison that provokes much intrigue and anticipation.

Pity   A time for humanity and kindness.

Placard   A need for greater confidence and exuberance.

Plague   An integral fear of poverty and affliction.

Plastic   Substitute; an alternative.

Play   Promotes participation in light-hearted activities.

Plead   To plead hints at the existence of hidden motives and deception; to see others pleading points to the revelation of covert activities.

Pleasure   Any form of pleasure denotes emotional fulfilment.

Pleasant   To find anything pleasant signifies an interesting and agreeable interlude.

Plough   A commitment that will eventually yield great rewards.

Plum   Relates to sexual appetite.

Poach   A need for closer scrutiny. Although this relates primarily to animals, given the frequent practice of 'play on words' by the subconscious, the meaning can also be applied to Egg.

Poetry   Emotional provocation.

Poison   False accusations; slander.

Police   Vigilance; caution.

Pond   A relationship that seems to be at a standstill.

Porcupine   Childlike innocence and playfulness.

Post   A desire for greater expression and communication.

Postcard   Signifies unexpected news from afar.

Potato   Represents basic essentials.

Poverty   Fear of emotional desolation.

Praise   To receive praise points to an overwhelming need for approval; to give praise recommends a more open-minded and unprejudiced attitude.

Pray   An indication of faith and belief.

Preach   A dissection of values and principles.

Pregnancy   Highlights a desire for change and improvement through new ideas and developments.

Present   To receive a present denotes an unexpected surprise; to give a present signifies renewed friendship.

Pride   Realisation of dreams and ambitions.

Priest   Spiritual advice and guidance.

Prince/Princess   Childhood aspirations.

Prize   Success after much hard work.

Promise   Urges an examination of issues concerning honour and integrity.

Proposal   An extremely significant liaison.

Prostitute   Relates to the hidden aspects of any given situation.

Public house   Leisurely pursuits.

Pudding   Innocent love.

Punch   Impulsive action.

Punishment   To apply punishment indicates selfish behaviour; to be punished is a sign of unnecessary sacrifice.

Purple   Psychic awareness; healing.

Purse   Financial transactions.

Push   To be pushed points to harmful levels of compliance; to push someone else warns against over confidence.

Puzzle   A deceptive set of circumstances.

Pyramid   Hidden mystery.

Q

Quaker Represents alliance and affinity.

Quarantine Highlights the need to withdraw from a potentially damaging situation.

Quarrel Depicts conflictive views and divided loyalties.

Quartz A situation that requires greater precision and transparency.

Quay Signifies change and transition within a relationship.

Queen Female hierarchy and dominance.

Question Hidden, unresolved issues.

Queue The importance of patience is emphasised.

Quibble A warning against futile disputes.

Quick Any quickness in motion refers to excitement and emotional fulfilment.

Quicksand Danger of being consumed.

Quiet Denotes a yearning for greater peace and calm.

Quilt An indication of warmth and security.

Quit Impetuous behaviour; thoughtlessness.

Quiver Provocation; incitement.

Quiz Dilemma; quandary.

R

Rabbit   An indication of dread and fear.

Race   Whether observing or participating in any racing event, the suggestion is one of competitive conditions that require imagination and stamina.

Raccoon   Generosity.

Radio   Points to undercurrent; a need to read between the lines.

Rag   To be seen wearing rags refers to a sense of inadequacy, especially within the social arena; to see others in rags emphasises the necessity for greater social adjustment.

Railway   The beginning of change and transformation.

Rain   Cleansing; washing away negativity.

Rainbow   Refers to a feeling of calm after the storm.

Rake   Gathering data for a particular purpose.

Rash   A negative emotional reaction.

Rat   Objectionable behaviour.

Raven   To see a raven denotes the beginning of a special and magical period of change and development; to see the colour raven (as in raven black) points to feelings of intrigue and curiosity and almost takes on some of the magical qualities of the raven with an emphasis on the emotional elements of the situation.

Razor   A need to be more sharp and astute.

Read   An indication of longing for greater knowledge, usually with an emphasis on a particular subject matter.

Rebel   A conflict of opinion.

Reconcile   Reaching for inner peace and balance.

Red   Passion; instinctive energy.

Reflection   The truth.

Refuse   A time to exercise assertion in order to achieve an acceptable outcome.

Regiment   A desire for greater unity.

Rehearse   Confidence building; encouragement.

Reincarnation   A sense of reawakening and revival.

Release   Promotes a more open and honest route where communication is concerned.

Religion   An analysis of spiritual knowledge.

Remove   Any form of removal recommends an alteration as regards current plans.

Rent   To rent something or to pay rent denotes temporary conditions that will eventually come to an end; to have difficulty in paying rent is a sign of impatience.

Rescue   To be rescued in a dream points to unexpected assistance that proves invaluable; to attempt a rescue

suggests a willingness to initiate reconciliation where there has been discord and disharmony.

Resign Inevitable change that may prove emotionally provocative.

Resist To resist or be aware of resistance in a dream signifies a situation that has lost balance and perspective.

Resolve Depicts a positive outcome through perseverance and careful analysis.

Respect Any issues surrounding respect refer to ambitions, particularly in relation to public image and persona.

Rest A much-awaited holiday.

Restaurant Social gatherings.

Resurrect A sign of renewed zeal and ambition.

Retire The end of a significant cycle.

Revenge Feelings of anger and resentment.

Revolution Much movement and commotion that would consequently lead to change.

Reward Signifies a sense of pride and accomplishment.

Ribbon Frivolous fun.

Rich To be aware of riches indicates that hard work and determination can initiate gain and reward.

Riddle Represents doubts and uncertainty as regards an emotional situation.

Ride A desire to gain control and re-establish power.

Ring Fidelity and commitment within a relationship; marriage.

Riot Disruptive external circumstances.

Rival Denotes immense animosity and mistrust and a need to confront long-held insecurities.

River Emotionally charged thoughts and conditions.

Road The journey through life.

Rock A yearning for security and stability.

Rocket A desire to break through boundaries.

Roof Feelings of self-preservation.

Room This can represent an aspect of the personality as well as thought and attitudes in general. In the setting of a house, different rooms relate to different areas. The kitchen refers to domestic matters and depending on other details, focuses on aspirations or problems in this area. The dining room is associated with family values and traditions; the sitting room with purpose and ambition. The emphasis on the bedroom lies on love and relationship issues. Depending on the context, the bathroom can deal with a variety of issues, however, in all cases it revolves around the need to cleanse and dispose of a particular situation to proceed to the next level. The basement area primarily relates to hidden fears and inhibitions. With the attic, the focus lies on the importance of recreational activities.

Root Stability.

Rope Searching for an escape.

Rosary Contemplation; meditation.

Rose A token of love and affection.

Rot To see something rotting suggests that swift action needs to be taken to initiate a productive change in the current course of events.

Row Physical exertion.

Royal Any royal connotations in a dream refer to aspirations and objectives that have not yet been put into motion.

Rubbish A suggestion to clear your space of unnecessary clutter.

Rug Seeking material comforts.

Run An indication of obstacles that need to be overcome.

Rust Neglect; carelessness.

S

Sack Indicates hidden elements.
Sacrifice An examination of motives; searching for a higher purpose.
Saddle The seat of power; an ambitious venture.
Sad Low morale.
Sail The emphasis lies within an emotional adventure.
Saint Signifies an inner appreciation of the real values of life.
Salad A time for carefree fun and enjoyment.
Salary Highlights a significant review of financial options and possibilities.
Salt An indication of material wellbeing; commodity.
Salmon Denotes an inner sense of knowing.
Sand This is a reference to the influence of time as regards a particular situation.
Sandals Relates to financial issues and in particular highlights conditions that require greater flexibility and liberation from a monetary perspective.
Sapphire A token offering of love and affection.
Satin An appreciation of feminine aspects.
Savage Any situation depicting savage behaviour refers to unusual or secret desires.
Scab Emotional wounds that have not yet healed completely.

Scald A serious warning, depicting unexpected setbacks and disruptive interference.
School Refers to knowledge that can be fully understood and absorbed with time and dedication.
Science Recommends a more coherent and logical approach as regards certain problems.
Scissors A decision whether to end or remould an existing relationship
Scratch An initial achievement.
Scream A longing to be relieved of tension.
Sea Represents the emotions experienced within any given situation.
Secret An anxious fear of the unknown.
Separate To separate from anything in a dream is an indication of emotional detachment.
Sew A sign of constructive undertakings and endeavours.
Shadow A complex symbol that primarily deals with alternative views within a particular situation; however, depending on the other elements involved, it can also refer to certain aspects of the personality.
Shark Relates to a potentially dangerous business involvement that may require much strategy and deliberation.
Shave Recommends an elimination of clutter and unnecessary elements.

Shawl   Generally, the presence of a shawl refers to social advancement.

Sheep   A need to be more decisive and proactive.

Shelf   To put anything on a shelf indicates a break from an ongoing situation; to notice things on a shelf denotes a period of reflection; to merely see a shelf recommends a change in tactics.

Shell   Protection; barrier.

Ship   Represents progression within a relationship.

Shirt   Ambition; objective.

Shiver   An emotionally-charged situation that can prove fatalistic.

Shoe   Generally shoes are indicative of financial conditions and material wellbeing.

Shoot   Any form of shooting seen in a dream is indicative of pending drastic action which may not necessarily prove favourable and should be avoided, if at all possible.

Shop   Represents choices and options as regards a particular situation.

Shoulder   Seeking courage and stamina.

Shower   Purification; starting afresh.

Sick   Any form of sickness is a sign of emotional difficulties.

Sigh   Pondering over past actions.

Sight   Refers to perception and observation.

Signal   A period filled with action and progress.

Signature   Identity; individuality.

Signpost   Recommends a cautious examination of all available information.

Silence   To be aware of silence within a situation refers to a period of thought and reflection followed by major decisions.

Silk   Material success.

Silver   Recommends a modest, humble demeanour regardless of success and achievement.

Sing   Should the singing be in tune, it denotes a satisfactory outcome to an emotional decision; singing that is out of tune or unpleasant is a sign of emotional uncertainty and dilemma.

Sink   To sink in a dream refers to serious problems that need to be addressed and tackled.

Sister   Representative of close female ties and relations.

Skate   An indication of rapid movement and progression.

Skeleton   The 'bare bones' of a situation; the essence of what truly counts.

Skin   Awareness; An acuteness of the senses.

Skunk   Worries around reputation.

Sky   An awareness and understanding of what lies ahead.

Sleep   Promotes a much needed pause from a tense and vexing situation.

Slippers   Domestic security.

Smell   To be aware of a pleasant smell denotes joy and gratification; an offensive smell points to a potentially damaging situation.

Smile   An extremely positive omen depicting accomplishment and approval.

Smoke   Much awaited news and correspondence.

Smuggle   Secretive overtures.

Snail   An emphasis on the application of patience and endurance.

Snake   False friends; betrayal.

Snow   Virtuous qualities.

Soap   A need for spiritual purification; redemption.

Soldier   Recommends greater discipline and commitment.

Sorrow   A sense of loss and regret.

Soup   A longing for family comforts.

South   Emotional contemplation.

Spear   A sign of pending disagreements and conflict.

Spell   Augurs an awakening of new and exciting sensations.

Spend   Financial review.

Spider   An interest in creativity.

Spin   Seeking spiritual enlightenment.

Spit   Contempt; disgust.

Sponge   A warning against overwhelming exposure to negativity and problems.

Sprain   Unavoidable setbacks.

Spring   Renewal; the beginning of a new chapter.

Spy   An unhealthy preoccupation with trivial matters.

Square   A desire for safety and security.

Squint   A warning not to ignore recent uncomfortable discoveries and revelations.

Squirrel   Promotes the importance of planning and gathering for future needs.

Stain   A damaged reputation through reckless behaviour.

Stairs   To go upstairs promotes a willingness to confront and surmount problematic situations; going downstairs highlights deep-rooted emotional insecurities that need time and patience to overcome.

Stammer   Frustration through emotional uncertainty and inadequate communication.

Stamp   Refers to a desire for a more personalised approach.

Star   An indication of hopes and dreams.

Station   Points to an extremely important and fateful period in time.

Steel   Depicts strength and courage.

Sting   Harmful rumours and gossip.

Stockings   Pleasurable pursuits.

Stone   Represents a variable that may affect current plans.

Storm   Signifies emotional upheaval and turbulence.

Stranger   An unrelated situation that may inadvertently prove important and influential.

Strangle   To be strangled denotes resentment and anger towards a situation that has been primarily based on power play and intimidation; to strangle someone warns against thoughtless and hasty behaviour that can prove regretful; to watch someone being strangled recommends a closer look at certain surrounding relationships where there may be uncomfortable questions as regards conduct and demeanour.

Strawberry   An enjoyment of sensual pleasure.

Street The emphasis lies on daily events and everyday routines and habits.

String An indication of time and its influence as regards a particular situation.

Strip A desire to liberate from restraints and inhibitions and yet fearing the consequences.

Struggle A danger of emotional fatigue and stress through pressure.

Stumble Better planning and organisation may be required to avoid delays.

Suffocate Feeling hindered and restricted.

Sugar Refers to a period of immense fun and pleasure.

Suicide Denotes defeat through an unfortunate lack of judgement.

Suitcase A much desired change of scenery.

Sulk Fear of disapproval and rejection.

Summer Positive energy and prowess; virility.

Summons This is a reference to an ongoing disagreement that may require external involvement before a satisfactory resolution can be attained.

Sun Masculine aspects.

Swamp A warning against being used and taken advantage of in an already charged and challenging situation.

Swan An indication of faith and hope.

Sweet Whether eating sweets or tasting something sweet, the connotation is that of an extremely serious relationship that can lead to marriage.

Swell Any form of swelling is an indication of overwhelming emotional anxiety that has not yet been resolved.

Swim To be swimming comfortably is indicative of emotional happiness and satisfaction; to experience difficulty in swimming points to conflict in relationships.

Swing Indecision; doubt.

Sword A sign of power and ambition.

Synagogue An appreciation of traditional spiritual beliefs.

Syrup Denotes a sweet and passionate love affair.

𝒯

Table Purpose; intention.

Tablecloth Represents views and ideas in relation to existing plans.

Tail Extra caution and vigilance is recommended, particularly as regards a sensitive subject matter.

Tailor A need to reassess current strategies.

Talisman Searching for answers in an attempt to resolve emotional issues.

Talk Advice; recommendation.

Tame Any attempt to tame an animal is indicative of inner conflict and indecision.

Tangle Points to unexpected disagreements.

Tantrum Denotes emotional anxiety and a sense of burden.

Tapestry An enjoyment of creative skills and activities.

Tattoo A desire for greater expression and individuality.

Tax Relates to financial responsibilities.

Taxi Career advancement through external influences.

Tea Looking towards tradition for answers to current questions.

Teacher Highlights the lessons learnt through life.

Team Any form of teamwork or activity promotes success through unselfish behaviour.

Tear To see tears in a dream suggests emotional release and freedom.

Tease To be teased points to hints and nuances that need to be examined and adhered to; to tease someone signifies difficulties in expressing purpose and intention.

Telegram This relates to some form of correspondence or conversation that may have taken place some time ago, but one which can prove instrumental as regards a current decision.

Telephone Refers to encounters and meetings.

Telescope A desire to look beyond the obvious; exploration.

Television Depicts activity and movement in conjunction with new information.

Temple Promotes greater spiritual interest and involvement.

Temptation An emotional situation that may not be all it seems.

Tent Basic needs and requirements.

Terrace Façade; external appearance.

Terror Denotes unforeseen events that can cause much upheaval and disruption.

Thaw Recommends a softer, more flexible approach towards an ongoing situation.

Theatre Emphasises a certain emotional episode which has remained significant.

Theft To witness theft is an indication of unexpected betrayal;

to be involved in theft warns against hasty judgement and irrational behaviour.

Thermometer Refers to moods and disposition.

Thigh Sensual desires.

Thimble A need for protection against minor ailments.

Thin Any form of unusual thinness depicts insecurities that can lead to neglect and a loss of control.

Thirst Denotes an intellectual awakening.

Thorn Points to petty irritations and annoyances.

Thrash Sulkiness; immaturity.

Thread Refers to important clues that should be observed and taken into consideration.

Threat To feel threatened in a dream is an indication of unexpected setbacks and competition accompanied by devious, underhanded behaviour; to threaten someone warns against poor judgement and unfortunate consequences.

Throat Highlights speech and expression.

Throne A desire to combat all existing problems.

Thumb Depicts flexibility and movement.

Thunder Major arguments and disputes.

Tiara An important introduction.

Ticket A life-changing opportunity.

Tickle Childhood pleasures.

Tide Refers to the sensations and feelings experienced within a relationship.

Tiger Denotes great strength and independence.

Tile An over-view of plans and objectives.

Till Relates to unexpected expenditure.

Timber Recommends greater reflection as regards future prospects.

Time To be aware of time emphasises the need to pay closer attention to the sequence of events. This in turn should clarify any associated relevance in relation to the achievement of goals and objectives.

Tin Financial difficulties.

Toast Points to matters involving daily routine.

Tobacco Male bonding.

Tomato Points to versatility and resourcefulness, especially in domestic matters.

Tomb Signifies an acceptance of change.

Tongue The emphasis lies with language and communication.

Tool Promotes greater exploration and understanding of natural skills and talents.

Tooth Refers to health matters; beautiful teeth indicates excellent health; decaying teeth point to health issues that need attention; to lose teeth is a warning not to neglect any health-related problems and worries.

Torch A search for clarity where there has been turmoil and confusion.

Tornado Highlights an extremely volatile relationship.

Tortoise   Gentleness; peaceful disposition.

Torture   To be tortured points to feelings of guilt and remorse that need to be analysed and dealt with correctly; to torture someone else is an indication of overwhelming anger and resentment that has proved overwhelming and unbearable.

Tournament   Healthy competition.

Towel   Depicts self-care and pampering.

Tower   A major challenge.

Town   Points to a busy period filled with excitement and new opportunities.

Toy   Light-hearted endeavours.

Trade   Signifies a mutually beneficial interaction.

Traffic   Unexpected delays and interruptions.

Tragedy   Depicts unsettling personal issues that have not been addressed.

Train   Refers to an event of major significance.

Tramp   A warning not to pass judgment without understanding all relevant facts.

Trap   Danger of insincerity and false promises.

Trapeze   Highlights the need to be more flexible and adaptable.

Travel   A sign of movement and change.

Treachery   Any form of treachery is indicative of inappropriate behaviour and superficial motives.

Treacle   Innocent love.

Treasure   A significant discovery.

Tree   Represents the passage of time and its effect in terms of achievement within a given situation.

Trespass   The emphasis lies with emotional boundaries.

Tug   Highlights emotional interaction.

Tulip   Represents a long-distance love affair.

Tumour   Signifies overwhelming emotional distress and anxiety.

Tunnel   Denotes constraints and difficulties.

Turnip   Reflects a need to get to the root of a matter.

Turtle   Success through wisdom and patience.

𝒰

Ugly   To feel ugly in a dream warns against unreasonable self-criticism; to see ugliness in others recommends better insight into the true characters of certain individuals.

Ulcer   Represents continuous irritations through neglect.

Umbrella   A need for greater observation and preparation.

Unconscious   Denial; difficulty in facing and accepting the truth.

Unconventional   This refers to a longing for greater variety and new interests.

Undertaker   Denotes the end of an episode and the beginning of a new cycle.

Undress   Liberation; an expression of true desires.

Unfaithful   To be unfaithful warns against an unwise decision that could end in regret; should someone else be unfaithful, a closer examination of motives and intentions within an ongoing situation is recommended.

Unicorn   A wonderful omen, denoting dedication and courage.

Uniform   Represents commitment and responsibility.

Unity   Any form of unity in a dream is a sign of optimistic interaction.

University   An interest in higher spiritual knowledge.

Unlock   To unlock anything easily denotes success and a favourable resolution to current plans and projects; should the process prove difficult, new or revised strategies may be required.

Uproar   Points to a restless and uneasy period.

Upset   An indication of disruptions and upheaval.

Urine   Recommends a reassessment of financial issues.

Vaccinate Preventative measures are recommended as regards certain business transactions.

Valentine A desire for greater expression of love and affection.

Valley Represents inner emotional hopes and wishes.

Vampire A warning against excessive negativity and pessimism.

Van Refers to any business-related activity.

Vanish Signifies a yearning for greater financial liberation.

Vanity A dubious friendship.

Vase A beautiful vase points to emotional stability and contentment; should the vase appear damaged or broken, there is a danger of restlessness and feelings of insecurity.

Vault An indication of secrets and mysteries.

Veil Denotes interference and insincerity.

Vein Life-changing decisions.

Velvet An enjoyment of beauty and refinement.

Ventriloquist Signifies lies and falsehood.

Verdict Highlights the outcome of an important decision.

Vermin Represents disruptive influences.

Vertigo A need to take a closer look at long-held fears and obsessions.

Vet Emphasises the need for greater spiritual healing.

Victory Points to success after much struggle and hardship.

Village A more relaxed and natural lifestyle is recommended.

Villain Destructive intentions and malice.

Vinegar Points to 'sour grapes' and resentment.

Violence Signifies conflict and anger.

Violet Psychic awakening; intuition.

Vision Insight; awareness.

Vocabulary Highlights dialogue and communication issues.

Voice Refers to correspondence of a personal nature.

Volcano A sign of ardour and passion.

Vomit Points to an emotional situation that has become insufferable.

Voodoo Looking for answers in unusual places.

Vote A desire for individuality and distinction.

Vulgar Any form of vulgarity signifies questionable motives in relation to a love affair.

Vulture Dangerous pursuits.

Waist   Presentation; appearance.

Walk   Represents pace and movement through events and situations.

Wall   An indication of barriers and division.

Wallet   A reflection of approach and attitude where financial matters are concerned.

Wander   To roam aimlessly denotes a period of distress and confusion.

War   A sign of rivalry and conflict within the business arena.

Warehouse   Points to past decisions and options.

Wart   An unpleasant incident.

Wash   Represents a need for emotional cleansing and the necessity to start afresh.

Waste   Selfishness.

Watch   An emphasis on time as regards current activities.

Water   An indication of the flow of feelings and sensations within a relationship.

Waterfall   An abundance of emotional expression.

Watermill   A need to work harder to resolve any emotional issues surrounding an existing relationship.

Wave   Stirrings of the heart.

Weave   Highlights the complexities within a particular situation.

Web   A desire for greater scope and development.

Weigh   A more rational and democratic attitude towards an ongoing dilemma is recommended.

West   Relates to intellectual and career issues.

Whale   Inner understanding; natural wisdom.

Wheat   Basic essentials.

Wheel   Setting plans into motion.

Whip   A waning against unnecessary force and constraint.

Whirlwind   Points to an all-consuming emotional event.

Whisper   Rumour; gossip.

Whistle   Hidden messages.

Widow   Denotes loss and heartache.

Wife   Highlights female issues within a relationship.

Wig   Image; presentation.

Wilderness   Having to start from scratch.

Will   An emphasis on the need for greater management and organisation.

Wind   Agitation; provocation.

Windmill   Depicts movement and advancement within a relationship.

Window   Points to an opportunity.

Wine   An appreciation of traditional values.

Wing   Looking for a way out of a potentially harmful situation.

Wink   A sign of fun and flirtatiousness.

Winter   Conclusion; resolution.

Witch   Fear of the unknown.

Witness Highlights the need for greater observation and scrutiny.

Wizard Unusual ability.

Wolf Psychic influence; intuition.

Woman Represents feminine influences.

Wood Signifies natural skills and talents; resourcefulness.

Wool An indication of warmth and comfort.

Work Refers to ambition and productivity.

Worm Change; renewal.

Worry Points to conditions that can prove troublesome and distressful.

Worship An examination of true inner needs.

Wound A sign of emotional disappointment and separation.

Wreck Major disruptions.

Wrestle Friendly rivalry.

Wrinkle Experience; wisdom.

Write A clearer understanding of motives and attitudes would prove highly beneficial.

𝒳 𝒴 𝒵

Xenophobia Points to dangerous and harmful decisions.
X-ray An important revelation with a surprising outcome.
Xylophone *See* Music.

Yacht An indication of material wellbeing within a relationship.
Yawn Feelings of stagnation and boredom.
Yearn Points to long-held hopes and wishes.
Yeast An interest in new challenges; rising to the occasion.
Yell Signifies frustration and inhibition.
Yellow An optimistic outlook.
Yield Long-awaited results.

Yolk The essential element; the nucleus of a situation.
Youth Denotes enthusiasm and fresh pursuits.

Zebra Opposing points of view.
Zigzag Denotes a need for diversification.
Zinc Outward appearances; the finishing touch.
Zip An opening; opportunity.
Zodiac Signifies an unexpected source of information.
Zombie Insincere and harmful advice.
Zoo Promotes greater attention to surrounding conditions.

Index

labels 56, 57, 58
Laura's dream 61–65
letter 56, 57
linen 56, 57, 58
lion 14
literature, references in 15
love 17
lust 17

man 29
mannerisms 15
mathematics 63
mattress 24
memory, hidden 44–47
mine 14
monster 63, 64
mother 41, 42, 43
music 27, 28, 45, 46
mystery 44

nails 37, 40
naked 56, 58
name 60
narrative: manipulated 52–55;
prophetic 50
nausea 22, 25
nest 37, 39
newspaper 37
night 23
nightmares 9, 55–63;
psychological 56–60;
recurring 61–65
nod 37, 38

obsessive compulsive disorder
56, 59, 60
offend 37, 38, 39
office 29, 30, 61, 63
old 25
optimism 31

pain 17, 62
paper 56, 57
paralysis 61–64
partial definition 48

path 22
Paul's dream 37–40
pen 56, 57
perfume 56, 57
phobias 16, 55
photographs 41, 42
physical and environmental
conditions, dreams
prompted by 9, 47–49
pill 61–63
pillow 214
pleasant 33, 35
pond 23
predictive dreams 9, 49–55
premonition 9
psychic ability 50
psychological: dreams 8, 21–36;
issues 13

questions 33

rabbit 37, 39
read 37, 38
rebel 37, 38, 39
recurring dreams 8, 37–47,
55
red 22–24
religion, references in 15
rival 34
robbers 45, 46
Robert's dream 56–60
roof 37, 39
room 24
rose 22, 25–26
rotting 22, 25–26
run 59

Samantha's dream 41–44
sandals 45
scissors 41, 42, 43
sequence: of events 20–21;
of images 47
serpent see snake
sexual undertones 54
shop 29, 30

sick 59
silence 33, 35
sing 46
sister 27, 28
skates 45
smell 22, 25–26, 56, 57
snake 14, 15, 17, 20
social interaction 15
spit 37, 38, 39
square 40
stairs 24
station 33, 34, 53
strangle 46
stress 8
subconscious 8, 14, 28, 32,
36, 37, 47, 49, 52, 53–55,
59, 60, 64
superstition 14
swan 22, 23
sword 37, 39
symbols 12, 20; as analogies
13; formulisation of 16;
symbolic representation 54

table 215
talk 35
teeth 56–59
telephone 33, 35
television 41, 42, 53, 54
threat 29, 62
tickle 37, 38
train 33, 53
trauma 8, 16, 41–44

upset 27–29

vampire 61, 62
vocal elements 16

walk 22, 29
whisper 64
word association 13–14

yellow 31